MY CRY IS TO ALL THAT LIVE

Through dialogue between her images and New Testament stories, Mary Burke creates a bridge between our foremothers in radical discipleship and today's women, hungry for a nourishing spirituality in a fractured world and church.

Mary's deeply reflective icons build on tradition in order to re-imagine how these stories can resonate in new ways. This book will enrich every seeker of new pathways for the spirit.

Dr Claire Renkin,
Head of the Department of Christian Thought and History at Yarra Theological Union, University of Divinity.

When women step into the biblical world there should be a sign at the entrance, "Here be dragons," as mariners were once warned on ancient maps not to stray too far south of the known world.

The biblical text was created in a patriarchal world and presupposed that this is "god-ordained." It takes creative imagination to dive into the silence, the spaces around the words and perceive the shadowy figures of women, the daughters of Holy Wisdom as they also embody the divine being. So many of our words that speak of God's presence are grammatically feminine – *Ruah*, the Spirit-breath; *Shekinah*, the holy presence, and of course God's darling child *Sophia* – and yet, most God-images are male. A new imaging is required to free the truth that 'female and male' image God. In this book Mary Burke invites us to explore with her beyond the known, into the unknown; to listen to the words women could have spoken in their proclamation of Jesus. Her words slay the dragons that might otherwise trap women in the doldrums.

Mary Coloe, pbvm.
Associate Professor, Yarra theological Union, University of Divinity

The cry of Divine Wisdom is addressed "to all that live". This has always been so and yet the cry of Divine Wisdom has not always been heard as Wisdom for all. The human community has taken precedence over the other-than-human community and, for some three thousand years, male humans have dominated in ways that have suppressed the voices and the agency of women. Through a unique combination of iconography, gospel text, engagement with the scholarly literature and creative writing, Mary Burke gives voice to those whom the tradition has tended to silence. As its subtitle suggests, this wonderfully imaginative and deeply personal work offers an invaluable resource for reflection on the voices of women and Earth in the Christian gospel tradition, reflection that has the potential to lead to transformative action.

Veronica Lawson RSM PhD,
eco-feminist biblical scholar; author of The Blessing of Mercy: Bible Perspectives and Ecological Challenges.

This is a most interesting book. Beautiful icons begin each chapter, followed by gospel texts containing stories involving women. Mary uses modern biblical scholarship by having background details for each passage, often quoting prominent feminist scholars before presenting her reflections. These are very creative with various characters reflecting on the story using modern speech patterns and communication styles, often in the first person or in reported speech. The characters include Kindness, Gabriel, Donkey, Death and Frog, reflecting Mary's interest in eco-spirituality.

This is a great resource about women in the gospels for all people who may not have time to read biblical commentaries. Mary's creative approach makes it easy to pick up and read, and contains great insights and wisdom. It provides teachers of Scripture in schools with models of different approaches to reflecting on gospel passages.

Dr Rose-Marie Prosser
Department of Theology, Mission and Ministry,
Yarra Theological Union, University of Divinity

MY CRY IS TO ALL THAT LIVE

MARY R. BURKE

COVENTRY PRESS

Published in Australia by
Coventry Press
33 Scoresby Road
Bayswater Vic. 3153
Australia

ISBN 9780648566182

Cataloguing-in-Publication entry is available from the National Library of Australia http://catalogue.nla.gov.au/.

Cover design by Ian James - www.jgd.com.au
Text design by Megan Low - FSG (Film Shot Graphics)

Typeset in Comorant Garamond size 12 on 17pts

Printed in Australia

Contents

Dedication

to Harry and Rose Burke
who gave me the precious gifts of life, family,
and entry into the Christian faith tradition.

Acknowledgments

First, I would like to acknowledge the Wurundjeri people on whose land this book has taken shape. I offer respect to their leaders, past and present and thank them for the care they have taken for this land over millennia.

I gladly acknowledge Veronica Lawson whose initial encouragement launched me on the road of finding my own voice with these stories; and Hugh McGinlay for his enthusiasm for the project and ongoing support.

Thanks also to those who gave their time and skills in reading, correcting and improving the written text: Irene Burke, Erika Smith, Claire Renkin.

A special thanks to those whose endless support and encouragement in this work and in life generally is always received with great wonder and appreciation: my sisters Anne Carr, Carmel York, Irene Burke and Marie Tonitto, together with Bernadette Wallis, Stancea Vichie, Judy Dynan and Bruce Duncan.

Thanks to Linda Price as Provincial of the Franciscan Missionaries of Mary — and to my FMM sisters for their ongoing support in this ministry of iconography and its Gospel message for today.

Icon of Sophia/Wisdom at play with God in the creation of the world.

PREFACE

Have you heard of Lilith?

According to the Alphabet of Ben Sira in Jewish folklore, she was Adam's first wife but the couple fought all the time. They didn't see eye-to-eye on matters of sex because Adam always wanted to be on top while Lilith also wanted a turn in the dominant sexual position. When they could not agree, Lilith decided to leave Adam. She uttered God's name and flew into the air, leaving Adam alone in the Garden of Eden.

> *Lilith, the first*
> *woman, created equal to Adam*
> *refused to lie under him.*
> *God, said Adam,*
> *make me a woman*
> *who will do as I say*
> *this woman you have*
> *given to me refuses*
> *to obey me*
> *she has her own will*
> *she is strong and evil.*
> *God listened to Adam*
> *and then*
> *there was Eve*
> *Lilith climbed the garden*
> *wall hardly looking back*
> *cursed by Adam*
> *she fell into the night*
> *whispering and calling*
> *the Eves across the centuries,*
> *Yes –*
> *you are equal – listen*
> *you are not of Adam's rib*
> *you are*[1]

The origins of this book lie in my experience of wanting to speak a word of hope, of meaning and of life to my sisters who have left the institutional Church, who have consciously or otherwise joined Lilith in her refusal to live under patriarchal rule. This word is both for them and for myself as I seek to live within our Catholic tradition, often on the margins and struggling with the oppressive structures of clericalism, hierarchy and their fallout.

Faced with a wide range of long held, sexist images of God, of life, in a period of time where wonderful women have left the Church in droves and witnessed by the apathy of Church hierarchy, I search for a simple way of exploring and holding alive some of the foundational Gospel stories that have kept Christians engaged creatively over two millennia, at levels of spirituality, social justice and politics.

Our ancient Scriptures have often been sources for the legitimisation of the oppression of both women and the earth. Their use as a patriarchal document has been called into play to uphold attitudes and behaviours that have led to a severe restriction on the flourishing of women and the natural environment. Women and nature have been lumped together and placed on a subordinate rung of the ladder of creation. This has had long term and significant impacts on the lives of women and the Earth, and in our day we are seeing in a stark way the impacts on the natural world around us.

Before plunging into this book, I invite you, the reader, to sit a while with another image... one older even than the stories we will read together... it is the image of Sophia (in English, Holy or Lady Wisdom).

This figure leaps out of our Scriptures at various points, a foil to the dominance of patriarchy. She is female, associated intimately with the divine being (we call God); she is filled with delight in the world and is a friend and companion of human beings. In fact, she is an image of the divine being in female form. The title of this book "My Cry is To All Who Live" comes from Proverbs 8:4 where Sophia calls out... "My cry is to all that live..." She calls out to all creation - human and non-human alike.

Elizabeth Johnson speaks of her thus:

> *Long-neglected texts in the biblical wisdom writings feature Sophia, Holy Wisdom, a divine figure of power and might. She shouts in the marketplace and at the city gates in a most unladylike manner, calling people to grow up, stop hurting each other, and walk in her path of justice. Playing in the world of creation, leading the Hebrew slaves over the deep waters of the Red Sea, sending her spirit as a blessing throughout the earth, spreading a banquet in which all are invited to partake, prevailing against evil, she is Israel's God in female imagery. Indeed her promise, "Whoever finds me finds life" (Proverbs 8:35) could be made by no one else.*[2]

She sits on the cover of this book in a prominent place because she will be our reading companion as we move through these pages. The image itself is taken from

Proverbs 8 where she is at play with God in the creation of the world. She is presented in icon form, sitting at the centre surrounded by the mythical seven days of creation, turned slightly, surveying, blessing and delighting in all she sees.

Icons are a particular 2-dimensional art form where the third dimension is in the eye of the beholder. Here, Sophia is depicted using the iconographic tradition in order to invite you into relationship with her, to feel her delight, wonder and joy in the world around her and its flourishing. She is an image of God who desires fullness of life for all that she has created.

We carry these divine sentiments with us as we approach each story. We will read and interpret them through two particular lenses, one is the experiences of women and the other is the current abuse of the Earth. And all the while we will be wondering and exploring how these stories might support the flourishing of women and the Earth today.

INTRODUCTION

In this book, we wish to listen once again to old familiar stories, to listen with new ears and be open to explore possible new meanings.

Why explore these stories?

As Jonathan Pageau says, "The world is held together by stories". It seems that from the beginnings of the human species, storytelling has formed the foundations of human culture, offering answers to ultimate questions or presenting unsolvable human dilemmas, all the while creating a web of meaning that shapes how we see ourselves and the world around us.

The stories in this work date back to the first century in the Christian era. They are the foundation stories of Western cultures and have held profound and world-shaping meanings for its audiences – for better or otherwise. As readers of this literature, we would like to pay attention to where these stories hit a chord or a dis-chord with us in the 21st century. How do we, reading through an eco-feminist lens, encounter these stories and what liberating meaning might we find in them? We may wonder, in fact, are they really 'good news' for women, for marginalised peoples, for the Earth in our world today? And if so, how?

Stories are always open to interpretation. The fact that they can be interpreted in various ways speaks of their depth and richness. In the work that follows, I will be using an eco-feminist critical approach. This is one way of approaching our Scriptures. It is not the only way. I have chosen this approach because it takes seriously women and Earth in all their differences.

The Bible, including the stories we explore here, is a literary artefact: books/stories written by men, for men and from a male experience of the world. They were also written in a male dominated cultural context and as such reflect that context, where the exclusion of women comes to be accepted as normal. It is important to hold this in mind so as to avoid the seduction of patriarchy which unconsciously affects us all. It has been and at many levels continues to be, the overarching world view of our culture and one which we have imbibed since our first breath.

As Elizabeth Schussler Fiorenza says – in the imagined voice of Herodias, the wife of Herod – "My sisters, I reach across the centuries to speak to you today: In your search for truth about women of the past, even women of biblical times – ***beware*** – because often what you find are stories by men about women."[1]

She also gives us a sense of the purpose of reclaiming these stories when she says:

> *A feminist reconstruction of Christian beginnings seeks to recover the past of women and other non-persons as a heritage for the present and a vision for a non-patriarchal future. The women who have shaped the early Christian movements are dead. After so many years we no longer can hear their stories and arguments. A feminist hermeneutics of remembrance desires to recover from historical silences the traces of their lives and faint echoes of their voices because of our need for a memory of women who have not only suffered and resisted patriarchal oppression but who have also spoken and acted in the power of the Spirit – Sophia.*[2]

The purpose of remembering and seeking to recover the voices and experiences of these women doing this is not just to recover an historical past but for the transformation of the present.

Patriarchal texts tend to erase the historical memory of the lives, work, feelings and struggles of women. By choosing stories from the Christian Scriptures that contain some mention of women, we need not be co-opted into believing that these texts are somehow different from traditional patriarchal texts. Rather, we will pay attention to Scripture scholars who through their work help us to hear the sub-text and parts of the story that have been relegated to forgetfulness. As Elizabeth Johnson says:

> *It becomes clear that the Word of God itself needs to be liberated into an inclusive world view in order to release its blessing for women.*[3]

In order to free the Word of God in the texts of the stories chosen in this work, I invite the reader to hold in mind four principles. This guide, drawn from Elizabeth Johnson's work, will help readers explore the liberating message often deeply buried in the patriarchal texts.

1. *Tip of the iceberg*: if women are mentioned at all, it indicates that they must have not only been there but to such an extent that they could not be written out of the story.
2. *How to interpret 'absence'*: if women are not mentioned, it does not automatically mean they were not present, e.g. at the Last Supper.
3. *Language*: women should be read inclusively into non-gendered words, so when male words are used meaning 'humanity', e.g. words like apostle, disciple, deacon, missionary, etc.

4. *The back story*: look for what might be happening behind the prescriptive statements. When rules are made, it often indicates that the opposite is actually happening and the rule is to prevent the behaviour. In First Corinthians, Paul says: 'Let women keep silent...' A feminist reading hears this as an indicator that women weren't keeping silent (and this was probably causing problems in the community).[4]

The layout of each story will include the scriptural text accompanied by an icon, some background thoughts from feminist Scripture and theology scholars and finally a reflection on the Scriptures.

We begin with texts from the Christian Scriptures. These are our sacred texts and as we are part of the living Tradition of the Church, we have the responsibility to hold and communicate them in ways that keep the Tradition alive and in conversation with the world and culture in which we live. This work is one simple attempt at doing that.

The version used is the *New Revised Standard Version* but occasionally I have highlighted certain words or phrases – these are terms that are significant in the commentary and reflection that follows. And once or twice, I have changed a word where the inserted term is used because of a certain theological emphasis I want to make.

Some of the icons that accompany the Scripture passages are traditional, well known icons while others have been created as there are no examples of them within the tradition, e.g. the woman with the lost coin or the persistent widow. Icons are a special form of religious art which has been kept alive by Eastern Orthodoxy and Catholic Churches of the Eastern Rite. Their use is mainly liturgical – as in the communal celebration of the Eucharist and other sacraments. However, they also form part of the personal prayer life of individuals and families. The icons in this book, then, are meant to stimulate personal and communal entry into the Scriptures at levels that may help deepen participation in the liturgy where this is appropriate, or to open a way to engage in new and fresh ways for those who are no longer connected to their particular Christian tradition.

The third section of each story offers a way of listening to female theologians and Scripture scholars as they attempt to engage attentively to the Scriptures from the perspective of women and Earth.

The Reflection Section has been done in the form of creative writing and so takes a certain liberty in expression and historical accuracy. Some of the stories invite more than one reflection. In these cases, I want to draw attention to the fact that there can be multiple interpretations and responses to the text. Its purpose is simply to stimulate thought on the part of the reader and possibly to invite the reader to enter imaginatively into their own critical reflections.

It should also be noted that this work offers a word regarding how our Scriptures may be read, interrogated and interpreted... one word among many. Speaking this word is a way of encouraging other 'words' to be spoken and explored.

Holding all these thoughts in mind, let us begin a little detective work and use creative imagination as we approach anew these ancient stories.

FOREMOTHERS OF JESUS

A modified family tree of Jesus, connecting him to his foremothers as well as to Mother Earth.

SCRIPTURE

Matthew 1:1-16

> An account of the genealogy of Jesus the Messiah, the son of David, the son of Abraham.
>
> Abraham was the father of Isaac, and Isaac the father of Jacob, and Jacob the father of Judah and his brothers, and Judah the father of Perez and Zerah by **Tamar**, and Perez the father of Hezron, and Hezron the father of Aram, and Aram the father of Aminadab, and Aminadab the father of Nahshon, and Nahshon the father of Salmon, and Salmon the father of Boaz by **Rahab**, and Boaz the father of Obed by **Ruth**, and Obed the father of Jesse, and Jesse the father of King David.
>
> And David was the father of Solomon by **the wife of Uriah,** and Solomon the father of Rehoboam, and Rehoboam the father of Abijah, and Abijah the father of Asaph, and Asaph the father of Jehoshaphat, and Jehoshaphat the father of Joram, and Joram the father of Uzziah, and Uzziah the father of Jotham, and Jotham the father of Ahaz, and Ahaz the father of Hezekiah, and Hezekiah the father of Manasseh, and Manasseh the father of Amos, and Amos the father of Josiah, and Josiah the father of Jechoniah and his brothers, at the time of the deportation to Babylon.
>
> And after the deportation to Babylon: Jechoniah was the father of Salathiel, and Salathiel the father of Zerubbabel, and Zerubbabel the father of Abiud, and Abiud the father of Eliakim, and Eliakim the father of Azor, and Azor the father of Zadok, and Zadok the father of Achim, and Achim the father of Eliud, and Eliud the father of Eleazar, and Eleazar the father of Matthan, and Matthan the father of Jacob, and Jacob the father of Joseph the husband of **Mary**, of whom Jesus was born, who is called the Messiah.

BACKGROUND

Let's take a moment to look at the icon above. The yellow ochre of the outer circle symbolises the gold of the divine presence. At the same time, it evokes the sun that brings light to the world. Out of the earth rise two mountains, earthy and sacred places of divine revelation. Jesus' throne is based on the flowering gum or *Corymbia ficifolia*, his footstool the earth itself, reminding us that Jesus and his forebears share with us a common origin in the elements that formed the universe. The tree is not simply a "family tree": it is the Tree of Life with its roots going deep down into the soil of Earth and into the very matter coming out of the origins of the universe. Jesus is surrounded by women - four are some of his foremothers. He is held in the arms of the fifth woman - his mother, Mary.

The icon bears the name "Foremothers of Jesus". The definite article is deliberately omitted because there is mention in Matthew's genealogy of only four of the many foremothers of Jesus. One is left wondering... where have all the other women gone? Jesus' foremothers were obviously as numerous as his forefathers. What has happened to Sarah, the mother of Isaac, to Rachel, the mother of Jacob, and to the thirty-four other unnamed mothers of male children who feature by name in this genealogy? Why include just four women in this predominantly male genealogy?

The image before us invites us to ponder these questions of exclusion and inclusion. It likewise invites us to ponder the choice of these particular women. What do we know of Tamar (Genesis 38), of Rahab (Joshua 2 and 6), of Ruth (Book of Ruth) and of the wife of Uriah (2 Samuel 11-12)? What do they have in common? There is no simple answer to that question, except to say that, like Mary, each of these women finds herself outside the patriarchial family structure and hence in danger. And in the face of danger, each one acted with courage and resourcefulness despite their vulnerability.[1] The Tradition also holds each one of these women as righteous, a term that indicates their good standing within the community.

Tamar, a childless widow, is the first woman to be mentioned. Tamar is married to Judah's eldest son, but he dies leaving her childless, and hence in a precarious situation socially and financially. She resorts to the Levirate Law (Deuteronomy 25:5-10.) which says if a man dies childless, his widow can demand sexual intercourse with the dead man's brother until she bears a son who will inherit the property that would have gone to the dead man, had he lived.

She then marries the second son, but he refuses to sleep with her because his share of the inheritance would be substantially less if Tamar produced a son. This second husband also dies leaving her childless once again. Judah has one more son but will not give him to her in marriage.

Tamar, however, will not be neglected or cast aside. Rather, she disguises herself as a prostitute and seduces Judah by the wayside. Falling pregnant to him and giving birth to twin boys, she achieved justice for herself even at the risk of being condemned to death by the unsuspecting Judah. The story of her liaison with her father-in-law, Judah, reveals Tamar's personal courage and initiative in the face of his cowardice towards her.

Rahab, Canaanite woman and sex-worker, places herself in danger in order to provide the Israelites with access to her land. She shelters Israelite spies who are gathering information prior to invading. In return for her help, Rahab achieves the safety of those she loves when the invasion happens, "a survivor in the world of men at war".[2] Within the genealogy, this Rahab is to become the second mother-in-law of Ruth.

Ruth, also a childless, poor and homeless widow, leaves her native country of Moab with her mother-in-law Naomi, on the death of her husband and brothers-in-law. As a widow and a foreigner, Ruth is doubly endangered. However, she uses her ingenuity to secure the protection of a husband. While he is sleeping, she crawls under the blanket of Boaz, a wealthy landowner of Bethlehem and brother of Elimelech, Naomi's late husband. She puts herself at risk of being condemned as a harlot by this behaviour but eventually is praised by her adopted people and finds her place in the family tree of the Messiah.

Bathsheba, wife of Uriah, attracts the eye of King David. In order to have her as his wife, David sends Uriah to the front line of battle knowing he will be killed. Among these women, she is probably the saddest. She loses her husband as a consequence of David's passion and whim, and, after falling pregnant to him, loses her first- born child. We hear nothing in this story about what Bathsheba wants, even her grief is silenced. Initially, she is the passive object of David's desire. It is only later in the story that we see her take initiative in securing the throne for her own son, Solomon. By this action, she secures her position socially and gains recognition as a foremother of Jesus in the unfolding story of God's engagement with the Jewish people.

It is interesting to note how these stories were written from a position of the male gaze and way of perceiving women in the world of men, and how their courage has fallen into forgetfulness.

Despite the inclusion of these women, there does seem to be a need to emphasise the male lineage of Jesus. One wonders whether this was the case because the social norms underpinning the patriarchal order were under threat. This may have been due both to the example of how Jesus and his early followers were living differently (e.g. Jesus' positive response to the poor and those on the margins, his attitude to the Law that brought freedom rather than bondage), as well as the stories regarding Jesus' manner of relating with women, with equality and mutuality, that were circulating in the community where Matthew was writing.

As well as highlighting the endless resourcefulness required of women living in a patriarchal culture, these four women play an active role in the revelation of God's presence in our world and foreshadow the role that the fifth woman is to play. Their presence in the genealogy functions "as a critique of patriarchy and introduces a note of tension into the narrative that must guide the reader as the story unfolds". [3] It also offers a critique of the male-centred world view underpinning it and poses a challenge to its power and control. This could be a link between these named foremothers and the final woman to be mentioned in the genealogy.

The fifth woman is Mary. She enters her son's genealogy only by virtue of her engagement to Joseph,[4] thus breaking the patriarchal pattern where the begetting and hence the line of descent comes through the male. In Matthew's Gospel, there is a hint of scandal in Mary's pregnancy which takes place before she comes to live with Joseph. Like the other foremothers, Mary finds herself outside the usual norms of patriarchal marriage and hence is vulnerable to social sanction and punishment. She is given no voice and no independent action, yet without her there would be no story![5]

So Mary's reproductive power outside patriarchal norms and her active role in the birth of the Christ is affirmed. It leaves us with an image of God as one who is not constrained by human systems of patriarchy and relates intimately with the grieving, the powerless and those on the margins.

Jesus' central position in the icon in the arms of his mother echoes God's presence with Mary, a marginalised and endangered woman in a male-centred world. It speaks of God's presence with all that are endangered in the human community and beyond.

The proverbial family tree symbolises the many generations that preceeded Jesus and its roots penetrate deep into the earth, reminding us of our intimate connection both with Earth and the whole universe which has its place in all our family trees.

Earth is represented in part by mountains which in iconographic language evoke the mountains where revelation took place e.g. Moses on Mt Sinai, Jesus on Mt Tabor. To the viewer, the presence of mountains says 'Pay attention! Something is being revealed to you here!'

REFLECTION

In praise of Mothers, Grandmothers, Foremothers... and, most importantly, Mother Earth!

Praise for mothers and all who give life to others,
For grandmothers (and grandfathers)

who bring the experience of life to the young
who have passed the age of worry and can delight in
and enjoy what life brings.
For great grandmothers and all our ancestors from ages past
without whom we would not be.
And for our Mother, Earth
who gives us food for body and soul
whose beauty entrances us
and in whose process of becoming we are a vital part.
Praise and blessing and thanksgiving!

Prayer of thanks for mothers

We thank you, Giver of Life, for all mothers and for mothering in all its guises. May our experience of being mothered, however that has happened, foster in us a deep sense of connection with all others who form the web of life with us, and a sense of our true place in the earth community. As we have been nurtured into fullness, may we too foster all forms of life around us, even when it appears small and seemingly insignificant. May those who are frightened, homeless or in danger find in us a sure help and a fierce protector. May our world flourish as you continue to mother it into being.

The Voice of Earth...

I sit here suspended in the darkness of the universe, spinning delicately, basking in the light and warmth of the sun. I have seen change, constant change, sometimes very slow and at other times so fast it leaves living forms in distress. I am Mother Earth. I hold the very matter of which you, to whom I address myself, are made. It is my flesh and when you are formed in your mother's womb you take on my flesh and grow to your fullness. You search out your ancestors to know who you are and where you have come from. But before your foremothers and forefathers, there was I, holding the seeds of your becoming, offering you the very ground from which you would emerge. Remember where you have come from, do not let the deepest truth of who you are as an Earth-being fall into forgetfulness. You do so at great risk - both for yourself and for me!

THE ANNUNCIATION

Icon of the Annunciation where a young woman opens herself to the Mystery of God.

SCRIPTURE

Luke 1:26-38

> In the sixth month the angel Gabriel was sent by God to a town in Galilee called Nazareth, to a virgin engaged to a man whose name was Joseph, of the house of David. The virgin's name was Mary.
>
> And he came to her and said, 'Greetings, favoured one! The Lord is with you.' But she was much perplexed by his words and pondered what sort of greeting this might be. The angel said to her, 'Do not be afraid, Mary, for you have found favour with God. And now, you will conceive in your womb and bear a son, and you will name him Jesus. He will be great, and will be called the Son of the Most High, and the Lord God will give him the throne of his ancestor David. He will reign over the house of Jacob forever, and of his kingdom there will be no end.'
>
> Mary said to the angel, 'How can this be, since I am a virgin?' The angel said to her, 'The Holy Spirit will come upon you, and the power of the Most High will overshadow you; therefore the child to be born will be holy; he will be called Son of God. And now, your relative Elizabeth in her old age has conceived a son; and this is the sixth month for her who was said to be barren. For nothing will be impossible with God.'
>
> Then Mary said, 'Here am I, the servant (**handmaid**) of the Lord; let it be with me according to your word.' Then the angel departed from her.

BACKGROUND

In Luke's story, we are told that the Angel Gabriel came to a virgin named Mary...

While virginity is by no means the central focus of this story, in preaching and popular discourse, the notion of Mary as a virgin giving birth has resulted in endless debates about the incredibility of such an event in the 'real' world.

The story of the conception of Jesus is first and foremost a theological statement, saying that Jesus' very being is from God, that somehow there is divinity here. As in other stories, it was not written as an historical text, so we cannot read this story literally.

Elizabeth Johnson takes up this notion of virginity and sees it as a symbol of female autonomy. She notes that in history a number of goddesses took lovers but were still considered to be virgin. These stories stress a paradox, a mystery; something other than the natural (biological) is being referred to in this paradox. This image of intersection of nature and divine leads Johnson to extend the definition of virginity beyond the biological in the following way:

> *"...to be virgins in the sense that they are free from male control, not accessories to men or dependent on their protection. To be virgin is to be one-in-yourself, free, independent, unsubordinated, unexploited, a woman never subdued. In this sense the virginal conception is valuable in bearing a message of revolutionary female empowerment."* [1]

However, Mary is pregnant, and in Matthew's account at least, there is some inkling that this pregnancy has a suspicion of illegitimacy, happening outside the patriarchal norms for women. And it is here, in the 'outside' place that the encounter with the Mystery we call God takes place.

Annunciation... here is a story of a young woman of seemingly low economic status and deeply rooted within her Jewish tradition. As such, we could assume that she shared the Jewish belief in God's compassion and desire for the freedom and fullness of life for her and her people. Like young women the world over, she is at that point in her life where she wonders what the future will be for her. She listens attentively to where life is taking her. In this context, she hears the call of God, expressed as a visitation from an angel, entrusting to her an unimaginable task. She will conceive and have a child. Mary's response follows the pattern of call stories throughout the Hebrew Scriptures which would have been familiar to Luke's audience. She questions the angel and takes time to reflect. Then she asserts her own autonomy and decides to take it on. She does not consult any male authority in this process. It is her own decision and it will shape her life from this point onwards. In this way, Mary engages with God's Spirit in her own life and shows how women of all time can do the same in their own lives.

The independent choice and action of Mary in this story has subversive implications. It validates the power of women to listen to God's Spirit in their lives. It offers women encouragement especially when they find themselves outside what is considered normative for women or feeling the backlash that usually follows when women take initiative or speak out in ways that challenge the status quo.

In a broader context, the subversion goes even further. This story of Mary's attentive engagement with God allowed God to take on human flesh – in fact all flesh (sarx) a reality that still blows our minds today! The Tradition calls this 'incarnation' and its radicality is explosive. It speaks of God's desire, God's uncontainable desire for relationship with us and with everything that exists. And what's more, that this relationship is written into our flesh, into our very DNA! It finds expression in the attraction of particles across space and time, in the drawing power of gravity and in the bonds that form among human beings, animals and beyond. There is nothing in the universe that is not drawn into this relationship.

In the unfolding life of the child that is taking form in the body of Mary, we will gain hints as to the nature of this relationship.

REFLECTION

Incarnation... more than we can conceive
the Mystery, the Source of all Being takes on flesh
real flesh, all flesh
nothing is left out, nothing excluded
human, animal, plant,
Earth itself
nothing
is
excluded.
Sophia, Wisdom,
– present at the creation of the world,
present when new life takes shape in the womb of Mary
present to us each day –
bows in profound awe
at Earth
at all flesh
transparent now with the living presence of God,
permeating everything
calling us to union, to life.
Sophia meets us
'...on the heights overlooking the road,

at the crossroads she takes her stand;
'I am calling to you, all people,
my words are addressed to all humanity. (Proverbs 8:1-6)
Which road will you take?
Will you tread one road with respect and wonder
or will you take the other
and trample, exploit, lay waste?
Each day I rise with you
each day I invite you
to celebrate
to enjoy
to be moved with awe
to reverence
each day
each day.

Gabriel

As he sat on the veranda overlooking the lake, Gabriel ordered a coffee and breathed a sigh of relief. It was done! His job today was a demanding one. Most days he visited ordinary people with simpler commissions – like to do an act of kindness, to forgive, or simply to be a slightly better person than they usually were. But there was a different feel about this one today.

He had been sent to a young woman on the cusp of adulthood to tell her that the child she was about to carry would be very close to the One her people called God. He would be seen as the one they were waiting for over these many centuries. He would show them how to live – that's if she accepted this proposal!

But he knew it would be more than that... Her openness to this One would not end in this particular moment, but would keep on being asked of her throughout her life. He didn't tell her all that, though. He wanted to get a good result and giving too much information usually didn't help his stats. He had learnt this over time and had honed his skills to get a better success rate.

The coffee helped to ground him and as he sipped, his thoughts continued to tumble one on top of another...

How would *he* respond to such an invitation? He smiled to himself at the thought and image of himself being pregnant! But as that thought faded, another took its place and stayed with him. 'I come and present people with these invitations to go beyond themselves, to hope, to strive, to long for more... and then I leave.'

It's one of the benefits of being an angel, he mused. He could drop these bombs and walk away. He never had to face the implications of what he delivered. That was for human beings to grapple with.

His mobile beeped... another job to be done! As he disappeared into the distance, there was a lightness to his step...another invitation to make, another chance to call someone to new heights, to inspire, encourage... easy-peasy!

Mary objects...

You will... you will... you will...

Ahhh, it's written as though I don't really have a choice! Yes I'm allowed to ask a few questions but really it's a forgone conclusion!

Well, let me tell you what really happened...

Gabriel came alright and spoke just as Luke has written. But I didn't answer yes at all... well, not quickly as it's told in the story! This was a pretty big ask of me and at first I was lost, didn't know what to say. So I said to Gabriel 'This is a big gig! Give me a bit of time to think this over.' He was cool about this and said he'd call again. It took me some time to make my decision... I had to think about how would Joseph deal with this if he didn't believe me? Then, of course, there was my parents' reaction! My answer would open me to a completely unknown future! Pretty scary!

Then I thought to myself... all our futures are unknown; Joseph's not a bad bloke and he thinks a lot of me, so that should be ok! Jacob and Anna... well, that's another thing, it will take a while for them to come around. But even more than all this, I had to sit with the question: Do **I** really want to get involved with all this? And I knew I had to make this decision on my own. I didn't want my father or Joseph telling me what I should do or think! This was my life and I wanted to choose what shape it would take.

So when Gabriel returned, I said, 'You're on!' None of this handmaid stuff!

The Meeting of Mary and Elizabeth

This icon is of the meeting of Mary and Elizabeth, two pregnant women praising God's compassionate love for the poor.

SCRIPTURE

Luke 1:39-56

In those days Mary set out and went with haste to a Judean town in the hill country, where she entered the house of Zechariah and Elizabeth. When Elizabeth heard Mary's greeting, the child leapt in her womb. And Elizabeth was filled with the Holy Spirit and exclaimed with a loud cry, 'Blessed are you among women, and blessed is the fruit of your womb. And why has this happened to me, that the mother of my Lord comes to me? For as soon as I heard the sound of your greeting the child in my womb leapt for joy. And blessed is she who believed that there would be a fulfilment of what was spoken to her by the Lord.'

And Mary said,
My soul proclaims your greatness, O my God,
And my spirit has rejoiced in you my Saviour,
For your regard has blessed me, a poor and a serving woman.
From this day all generations will call me blessed,
For you who are mighty, have made me great.
Most Holy is your Name.
Your mercy is on those who revere you throughout all generations.
You have shown strength with your arm
You have scattered the proud in the conceit of their hearts.
You have put down the mighty from their seat
and have lifted up the powerless.
You have filled the hungry with good things, and sent the rich away empty.
You, remembering your mercy, have helped your people Israel,
As you promised Abraham and Sarah, mercy to their children forever.[1]

And Mary remained with her for about three months and then returned to her home.

BACKGROUND

This story focuses our attention on two women: Elizabeth and Mary. Elizabeth is a Jewish woman faithful to her people's relationship with God. Living in a patriarchal culture, she is subject to a way of seeing that values a woman for her capacity to bear children, especially sons. She and her husband are childless which gives her both the social stigma and shame of being labelled as 'barren'.

In her advanced years, she has fallen pregnant and rejoices in what she sees as a blessing from God that brings both new life and lifts her shame. This joy overflows when she greets Mary and recognises God's blessing on her kinswoman also.

Mary greets Elizabeth with a powerful song put on her lips by the Gospel writer. It is in the form of a thanksgiving psalm, beginning with praising God and then naming what God has done to evoke such praise. Mary rejoices in how God's compassion and mercy have been experienced in her own life and then proclaims that this favour belongs to all the poor and lowly. This is the most that any woman says in Scripture! In the traditional silencing of women, this song calls for our attention both for the mere fact of it being on the lips of a woman as well as the sheer power of its message.

There are echoes in this song that hint of revolution. However, it is not a revolution in the ordinary sense where one power overthrows another and the same story continues with different players. The revolutionary outcome of this song is an order where there is equality and justice for the poor and oppressed; and one might add for the whole of creation. Elizabeth Johnson explains it thus...

> *This "preferential option for the poor signals who ought to get first attention because their suffering is so great. The motive for this divine preference is what gives new colour to the notion of God as holy mystery. This motive is nothing less than love, the free, gratuitous, unmerited character of divine love, which generously searches for those whom society marginalises and which elects to be in solidarity with the weak and abused of history."*[2]

There is an assumption underlying this call to revolution... it assumes that we hear this as a call to be engaged in the struggle to create a more just and compassionate world.

As Elizabeth Johnson notes, Mary

> *"takes on as her own the divine No to what crushes the lowly, stands up fearlessly and sings out that it will be overturned. No passivity here, but*

solidarity with divine outrage over the degradation of life and with the divine promise to repair the world."[3]

Johnson responds to this powerful story of two feisty women with a provocative question... "What has happened to the power of women in the Catholic tradition? How has this cutting edge voice of women been silenced within the halls of decision making and structural leadership?"

While the Scriptures present Mary preaching powerfully and with authority of the divine compassion, women in the Catholic Church still do not have the right to preach publically. This juxtaposition highlights the current scandal of the position of women in the Catholic Church today.

Just as women have been silenced down the centuries, so too have the voices of other-than-human creatures. As followers of the Christian God of mercy and compassion, we could ask ourselves a further question... Where are **our** voices being raised for those without a voice in the natural world as they face the onslaught of the insatiable appetite of human beings that is leading to their diminishment and even extinction?

REFLECTION

Breaking News from Jerusalem (reported on Skynews)

Reporter: This is John Burns reporting from Ein Karem.

Anchor: What's happening down there, John?

Reporter: Good evening, Dan. People on the ground here are claiming that two women prophets have been speaking out dangerously and with loud voices that can be heard all over the town! There is a younger woman, known in these parts as Mary. With her is an older woman who seems to be encouraging her to speak out. This older woman's name is Elizabeth and locals say that she is a tough one. Since she has fallen pregnant after years of barrenness, it's like she's got a real lease of power and authority. No one messes with her now, they say...

Anchor: So what are they doing that is causing such a stir?

Reporter: Yes, Dan. Ein Karem is in an uproar. Authorities here and throughout the occupied land are worried. These 'pregnant prophets', as people are calling them, are saying outrageous things like 'God will raise up the poor and cast down the rich'.

Can you imagine where this might lead? What would happen to the stock market! Our superannuation, our retirement, our holiday plans?

Anchor: My God! This is revolution in the making. There'll be a crack-down for sure. Where are their husbands? Is no-one there to take them in hand?

Reporter: No, it seems the men are not there. See what happens when women get together. They're causing havoc! 'God will feed the hungry and the rich will be sent away empty!' they say. This is subversive talk!

Anchor: How are they getting away with this?

Reporter: Well, Dan, the finance minister has come out to tell people to calm down. He says these 'bleeding hearts' are all talk and probably put up to it by disgruntled workers. He claims that the drive to accumulate wealth always trumps hopes for justice. He has launched the challenge to everyone: Do we **really** believe that God is on the side of the poor?

Anchor: Perhaps the Finance Minister is right. When have we ever seen God's preference for the poor? Certainly not in Federal budgets! The Minister's advice seems more realistic.

Reporter: Let these women rave on as they tend to do, he says, but pay them no attention. Keep adding to your investment portfolios and the Market is a surer source of help for us all!

This is John Burns reporting breaking news from Ein Karem.

This is the ABC evening news with Amal Khoury.

Heading the news tonight is a report from Ein Karem, 7 kilometres from Jerusalem.

In the midst of the news from around the world this week telling us of wild fires, earthquakes and battles of war, and at a time when religion and God are on the nose, comes a rather different story of two women who are making news in an extraordinary way. Drawing from their long, prophetic tradition, they are using all forms of media asking people to remember God's fidelity to the poor and those on the margins of our societies. They are saying that the financial system we have come to worship is simply not good enough, and that we are being called to something better. This new system they are advocating is one where the welfare of all human beings and Earth are kept centre stage. Centre stage in all our decisions, be they in business, in law, in education, in manufacturing, in agriculture... in all forms of human endeavour.

The National Business Council has responded in disbelief. Such a thing has not been heard of in the lifetime of their members. They have dismissed these women as being far too radical in the economic climate of today!

Women from around the world, however, have responded with enthusiasm. They are coming out onto the streets in places as diverse as Bangladesh to Zimbabwe, Scotland to Myanmar. They are carrying placards with slogans such as

'God is on the side of the poor!'

'The Earth deserves a better deal!'

"We're with Mary!"

'Thumbs up for God and a new deal for the poor!'

'Women calling for a fairer world!'

"An end to exploitation of the earth and its peoples!"

'God is with us!'

Commentators are saying that it has been a long time since we have seen a movement like this. Governments around the world are trying to play down the size of this uprising as it clearly threatens their hold on power.

The ABC will keep you informed about this stunning show of female power and solidarity as it unfolds. Stay tuned.

Gabriel

I'm off duty at the moment but this client has been such an interesting job for me I just want to see how she's going!

She's been a good investment in time really. She's causing a stir already and her pregnancy isn't even over yet!

Go girl! is what I say. Keep that feisty spirit... you're going to need it!

The Nativity

Mary and Jesus in conversation with the animals....

SCRIPTURE

Luke 2:1-20

In those days a decree went out from Emperor Augustus that all the world should be registered. This was the first registration and was taken while Quirinius was governor of Syria. All went to their own towns to be registered. Joseph also went from the town of Nazareth in Galilee to Judea, to the city of David called Bethlehem, because he was descended from the house and family of David. He went to be registered with Mary, to whom he was engaged and who was expecting a child. While they were there, the time came for her to deliver her child. And she gave birth to her firstborn son and wrapped him in bands of cloth, and laid him in a manger, because there was no place **(room)** for them in the inn.

In that region there were shepherds living in the fields, keeping watch over their flock by night. Then an angel of the Lord stood before them and the glory of the Lord shone around them, and they were terrified. But the angel said to them, 'Do not be afraid; for see – I am bringing you good news of great joy for all the people: to you is born this day in the city of David a Saviour, who is the Messiah, the Lord. This will be a sign for you: you will find a child wrapped in bands of cloth and lying in a manger.' And suddenly there was with the angel a multitude of the heavenly host, praising God and saying: 'Glory to God in the highest heaven, and on earth peace among those whom he favours.'

When the angels had left them and gone into heaven, the shepherds said to one another, 'Let us go now to Bethlehem and see this thing that has taken place, which the Lord has made known to us.' So they went with haste and found Mary and Joseph, and the child lying in the manger. When they saw this, they made known what had been told them about this child; and all who heard it were amazed at what the shepherds told them. But Mary treasured all these words and pondered them in her heart. The shepherds returned, glorifying and praising God for all they had heard and seen, as it had been told them.

BACKGROUND

Luke says quite simply 'she gave birth'. Underlying this phrase is the whole beautiful and terrifying experience of many women throughout the world and across time. Until recent times giving birth was a risky business for women, as complications could and often did result in the death of the woman or child or both. And in many places this remains true today. Any woman facing the experience of giving birth would have been aware of the risks involved, Mary included. It also draws our attention to an experience that Mary shares in common with women the world over who bring forth the life of another from their own bodies.

In this story, we see Mary and Joseph leaving their home and travelling a significant distance to comply with the demands of the Roman rulers. The background picture it opens up for us is one of a people under the occupation of a powerful empire, forced to pay taxes and obey the demands of the occupier in order to live any sort of peaceful life. Not unlike many people in the world of today!

Elizabeth Johnson reminds us of another connection that Mary has in this story with the experience of women in many places and times. She says that although the nativity is often presented in sweetness and light, the reality for this young woman was that basically she gives birth as a homeless woman. This is an experience that many women either know themselves or are aware that this could easily be their lot, given even a small change in their circumstances.

In Luke's simple yet packed sentence 'and she gave birth', he glosses over the actual birth process, leaving an impression that there was not much effort involved here, no mess, no blood, no sense that Mary would be in pain or the relief once the baby arrived.

The teaching of the early 'fathers' of the church further distanced Mary's experience of birth from other women's by claiming that Mary remained a virgin before, during and after this birth.[1] They were trying to speak of the divine origins of Jesus but in their attempts they stripped Mary of her womanhood and her sexuality, and as a by-product, demeaned that of all women.

The story ends with the words: 'Mary treasured all these things, and pondered them in her heart.' She mulls over what is happening in her life. Things are not as obvious to her as is often preached. Like most of us, she needs to reflect on where life is taking her, what meaning is there in her experience and what response is called from her?

We can approach the birth of Jesus from another angle. Theologians call this 'Incarnation' by which we mean God taking on flesh in Jesus. Among the many layers of meaning here let two come into focus for us... One is the use of the word 'sarx' which we translate as 'flesh'. This word holds meaning way beyond that of human flesh; it means all flesh in the created world! So, matter in all its forms becomes the place where God chooses to dwell and be encountered.

The second meaning that comes into focus is that taking on the sarx of the world, God is no longer sitting in a place of royal power but in the broken body of Christ crucified.

> *In light of the cross, feminist theologians reflect that sociologically it was probably better that the incarnation happened in a male human being. For if a woman had preached compassion and given the gift of herself even unto death, it would not have made a great impression. People expect women to serve. But for a man to live and die like this in a world of male privilege is to challenge the patriarchal ideal of male domination at its root.*[2]

God taking on 'flesh' not just a human body, but all flesh. It is an on-going process; it is the evolutionary process of the universe imbued with the active presence of God.

This birth takes place in the presence of animals, given the child is laid in a manger, a feeding trough for animals such as household beasts of burden. This detail can be overlooked or sweetened for children's stories. The connection with the world of the other than human is in our face and asks for our engagement. The icon for this section aims at drawing our attention to this reality in a simple way and invites us to reflect on what might be the implications for us if we allowed the lives around us–of all sorts– to be taken more seriously and be seen within our understanding of incarnation.

REFLECTION

A word from Mary, also known as the mother of God.

Women of the world. Let me share a word with you. You have heard many tales about me over the years. My life has not been my own. Worse even than the film and sports stars of today!

My son spent his life trying to show us something of what God is like and how this might shape the way we live. People gathered around him, forming community as people tend to do. But over time, this way of living became regulated by rules and structures, basically formed and controlled by the men of this movement. Women's voices didn't get much space or credence, so we ended up with some strange ideas. I have been the victim of these distortions, neglect and inflated claims. And worse still, I've been held up as a model for you! This model has robbed me of my husband and of my sexuality. It has taken my motherhood and glorified it beyond belief. You would think that I never raised my voice at my son or husband! That I never felt so tired I just wanted everyone to go away and leave me in peace!

Putting me on a pedestal has not only distorted my life, it has meant that ordinary women like you are seen as no match for me, as inferior and always second class! You have been set a goal that is unreachable!

Don't fall for it! We have, all of us, women and men, been made simple and fallible, no frills! I'm tired of this endless and senseless debate about whether I was a virgin! All such talk over the years has been grappling with how can we say that this man Jesus is divine? In fact, the divinity of Jesus is revealed in the quality of his humanity not in how I became pregnant! Let yourselves wrestle with that reality and leave me in peace!

Finally, let me say to you, women... yes and you men too! Keep a lively sense of suspicion when you hear groups of men speak, especially if it has anything to do with women, including myself! Use your own minds and intelligence. Listen to your deepest experience and trust it! Don't be led by your noses!

Conversation between the Cow and the Donkey

Cow: What's going on here today?

Donkey: We're getting visitors! You know there are so many humans in Bethlehem these days. Something's goin' on.

Cow: Oh, here comes a young woman; she's heavy with young. Oh God! Do you remember being that way too? It's a long time ago for me but the memory stays!

Donkey: Looks like her first. Poor one, her time is just about come.

Cow: She's calling out now in pain. Hope the little one comes quickly!

Donkey: Yes, here he comes! Humans are so feeble when they're born - takes them ages to mature and they wrap them up real tight!

Cow: Oh, but he's cute. Let's get a bit closer.

Donkey: Young woman, can we come close to see your newborn?

Cow: She's smiling at us so I guess it's OK.

Donkey: Go gently or you'll frighten him.

Cow: Isn't birth and new life incredible!

Donkey: Stop licking him!

Cow: I can't help it. There is something about this child, I feel it.

Donkey: Yes, I know what you mean. I want to dance and sing... it's like there's a joy in me that's bursting to come out!

Cow: Don't you get this feeling at every birth?

Lena's diary

January 18: I've just come back from the doctor's and she's confirmed my pregnancy!! I'm so excited and can't wait to tell Bill! Since our marriage six months ago he has been a bit touchy. Something is bothering him, but he won't talk about it; actually he doesn't talk much at all about what he's feeling. I think he'll be excited about this news though....

January 20: I got such a shock! When I told Bill that we were expecting he went right off! Began yelling at me and shoving me! Then he left the house saying he had to go for a drink.

April 29: I'm nearly six months now and starting to show. Bill has been ok since the last incident. I guess he needed time to adjust. He's not a bad guy really.

June 15: I'm at my parent's place. Bill came home last night in a bad mood. He started yelling and screaming at me and pulling me by my hair. At one point he called me a slut and punched me in the stomach. I was stunned. I escaped his ranting and went into the bathroom to gather my thoughts. I was in pain and anxious that his blow had hurt the baby. I was so upset I couldn't think straight. I played things coolly all evening until he fell asleep, then I took a few things and drove to my parents' place. My Dad is furious with Bill and Mum is so upset. I don't know what to do.

June 30: My waters broke while I was at my parents' place. They took me to hospital and I delivered a beautiful little boy. He's premature so will need some extra care. I wish Bill could have been with me... Dad says he's a controller and I guess he does like things his own way. I'm so disappointed... having my first child this way wasn't what I had imagined or ever thought would happen. Now, at the time when most women are enjoying this experience and sharing it with their partners, I'm here back at my parents' place and facing some very difficult decisions... it shouldn't be like this...

Anna the Prophet

An elderly woman voices hope for the people.

SCRIPTURE

Luke 2:36-38

> There was also a prophet, Anna the daughter of Phanuel, of the tribe of Asher. She was of a great age, having lived with her husband for seven years after their marriage, then as a widow to the age of eighty-four. She never left the temple but worshipped there with fasting and prayer night and day. At that moment she came, and began to praise God and to speak about the child to all who were looking for the redemption of Jerusalem.

BACKGROUND

Here is an eighty-four year old woman spreading the news of the Christ to all who came into the temple! Not relaxing in retirement, but on a mission in her old age!

She speaks out, not timidly but so that she can be heard and, in defiance of the usual behaviour expected of widows, she is doing this in a public place.

While widows were often seen as poor and vulnerable, this is not always the case. And here in the person of Anna we see another image – one of a woman who leaves her home and gives her days to fasting and prayer. This activity in Anna's life appears to have made her receptive and attentive to the activity of God around her and eager to speak of this child who will fulfil her people's hope for their future.

In Luke's Gospel, however, she is cast in the role of an Old Testament prophet. And while we are told of her activity, we do not hear her own voice, nor do we see others' reaction to her. Barbara Reid notes that by not giving Anna either a direct voice or audience, the Gospel writer encourages the reader to give her little notice.[1]

In this early part of Luke's Gospel, we are introduced to three strong and articulate women proclaiming the goodness of God as they experience it in their lives. (Mary, Elizabeth and Anna) The stories that follow, however, depict women crying out in need, and when they do venture something more, they are either corrected or disbelieved. It is not till we get to the end of the Gospel that we find once again stories about the fidelity, courage and depth of relationship among the women disciples, when we meet them, as they witness the execution of Jesus.

REFLECTION

Anna in the temple

The sun is shining as I walk through the colonnades of the temple. My movement is much slower now than when I first came to the temple as a young widow. In those days, I would move with ease and at a speed that was seen as lacking decorum!

But I take my time today and wend slowly towards the main doors of the temple as the morning crowd begin to arrive.

There is a song going round and round in my mind, so much so that I find I'm singing it softly to myself. *Avinu Malkeinu*[1] is an old song... old like me and well worn. There is something moving in it that touches me in a way I can't quite explain. Of course, some of the words for God I change... and I change them now as I sing to myself. 'Our Father, our King' are its opening words...but whenever I sing it, the words morph into 'Loving Father', sometimes into 'Compassionate Mother'. Today, it is the latter that I hear myself singing and feel my heart lifting. I am trying to remember the verses that are multiple, but in my old age only one remains in my memory. My steps slow down even further as I enter a quiet space within myself and sing...

> *Hear our prayer*
> *We have sinned before you*
> *Have compassion upon us and upon our children*
> *Help us bring an end to pestilence, war, and famine*
> *Cause all hate and oppression to vanish from the earth*
> *Inscribe us for blessing in the Book Of Life...*[2]

In my long years of life, I have seen many things, some so horrible I choose not to remember. My people and I are living under Roman occupation, an experience of daily harshness and, at times, of horror. With all my people, I long for a time of deliverance from this heavy burden.

As I sing my way to the opening of the temple I notice a new sense of hope rising within me...'Compassionate Mother...' Beginning the chant again, I look up and coming into the temple in the middle of the bustling crowd, I notice a young woman cradling an infant in her arms and a young man beside her carefully holding the pigeons for offering...

A pigeon finds her voice

I am one of the pigeons being carried by Joseph as he enters the temple. He has put me in a small cage with a companion. I have a feeling of dread as we move through the doorway. There is the smell of death here and my natural instinct to stay alive is making me very jittery! I take a deep breath and look round me. Mary is carrying her infant and there is an old man and an old woman both proclaiming something to the people gathered around them. They use strange words like 'salvation' and 'redemption'. I think they're talking about life in its fullness, but I'm feeling like mine will soon be emptied out!

This is no time to be philosophical… but… I guess I'm not the only animal to be sacrificed for the whims or beliefs of human beings! I wish I had a human voice so I could speak to them!

And what would I say?

I'd say, 'I want to live, don't kill me. Let me fly back to my flock and live as I was made to live….

'Please look further than yourselves and see that I too have a right to live.

'Do you think God desires my death as an offering? I'd be very surprised at that!'

Actually I think God would be rather puzzled by all this sacrificing stuff.

Flight into Egypt

Like so many families across the world today, this young family has to flee to safety.

SCRIPTURE

Matthew 2:13-15

> Now after they had left, an angel of the Lord appeared to Joseph in a dream and said, 'Get up, take the child and his mother, and flee into Egypt and remain there until I tell you; for Herod is about to search for the child to destroy him.' Then Joseph got up, took the child and his mother by night, and went to Egypt, and remained there until the death of Herod. This was to fulfil what had been spoken by the Lord through the prophet, 'Out of Egypt I have called my son.'

BACKGROUND

In Matthew's Gospel, the story surrounding Jesus' birth is told from the position of Joseph. Mary is voiceless and passive. Aware of this literary context, the story unfolds thus...

Joseph, Mary's husband, has a dream and in it he is warned that King Herod is threatened by the presence of a new-born whom he thinks will lay claim to his throne and is in **deadly** search for this child. As a protective parent, Joseph decides that they need to flee and without wasting time, he, Mary and the child escape into Egypt. The vulnerability and danger of this young mother and child are palpable and the urgency in the story propels them onto the road in the direction of the unknown.

The repetition of the phrase 'the child and his mother' paints a picture of the fragility and shared danger of the pair as well as the 'fierce care' the mother has for her child.

Like so many people across the world today and throughout the centuries, this young family finds itself facing dislocation and danger due to the violence of powerful men. Now they must trust themselves to the mercy of others in a foreign land. No extended family, no home, no job, in a land, a culture and language group not their own, they must start from scratch. Across history, how many other people have shared this experience, and especially today when there is one of the greatest movements of people internally and across borders due to war, political danger or natural disaster. There is also the often hidden dislocation of families due to domestic violence. In all these circumstances, it is always the poor, and particularly women and children, that are the most vulnerable and, like Mary and her infant, they rely on the mercy and kindness of others.

In the midst of this mammoth movement of peoples, ethnic and national boundaries are being challenged, the days of a mono-ethnic nation are fast disappearing. Our identity as human beings, how we see and understand ourselves is being stretched beyond what we have known and with which we have been comfortable. We are being asked to welcome into ourselves, our countries, our hearts those who have previously been seen as strangers, foreigners... to give them a place of belonging among ourselves.

And the stretching does not end there... at the same time as this huge human upheaval, there is also huge destruction of natural habitats, the extinction of countless species of animals and plants and Earth herself who, like refugees, cries out for mercy as its waters, land and air carry the unsustainable weight of pollution. We, who have traditionally seen ourselves as the pinnacle on the pyramid of creation, are being asked to step back and look afresh at who we really are in the intricate web of life.

All this is evoked for us in this simple icon of a woman, her husband and her infant in flight...

REFLECTION

Refugees across time and place

Joseph's story

I woke up in a sweat after a bad dream. It left me anxious and really disturbed!

The last few days of my life have been more than I can put into words. When Mary's time came, I was ushered out of sight by the midwife and the other women who gathered to help her. Being at a distance I could hear what was going on but couldn't see anything. All I could do was pace and worry. But when the little fella was placed in my arms, it was like all the lights went on for me. In what seemed like an instant I had become a father and I was well and truly smitten! A fierce sense of protectiveness came over me. I was responsible for him and his mother. In that moment, I became a man, an adult. And that's why my dream was so disturbing!

Living under occupation makes life hard in many ways, but, as a man, it has many humiliations. Not the least being a man's inability to keep his family safe. Gabriel came to me last night in my dream and warned me of Herod's plan to kill children of a certain age. He had some mad idea that they could eventually be a threat to his position of power. And Gabriel told me to flee into Egypt.

As I came to consciousness and saw Mary and the child lying beside me, my love for them and need to protect them from Herod's madness took hold of me. Even though this was well outside of my comfort zone, and still the middle of the night, I rose and began the preparations. By the time I returned, Mary had fed the baby and I talked with her about what we needed to do and we decided to leave as quickly as possible.

We are on the road now, going to a place neither of us knows. As I feel the earth under my feet and the sun on my back, I'm wondering.... how will these Egyptians treat us? We are of a different race and religion from them. Will they welcome us? Push us out? All I know is that we have no choice. For our family we must choose life and find a way to protect and nurture it.

I'm remembering the stories of our people when they were driven into exile in the past. I'm aware that I am not the first to make this decision and flee, and more than likely I won't be the last! Will we stay refugees? Will we ever go home?

Nadia's story

My name is Nadia. I am a Yazidi woman, living in a tent for the last three years away from my home. We fled the brutality of ISIS under the cameras of the world. But now no one thinks of us. We have gone off the front page of the newspapers as if all our problems have been solved! But we are stranded in a no man's land. It is not safe to return home and there is nowhere for us to go. We have no proper sanitation or clean drinking water. The rains are about to start and we will live in a sea of mud, if our shanties remain intact. Yes, we would flee like your Mary and Joseph, but no one wants us! Not even those in the West who stirred up this trouble in our country! And we are not the only ones in this position. What about the Rohingya in Myanmar, the Uyghurs of China, the people of Yemen and Syria, the Palestinians of Gaza and the West Bank… and so many others? Are we not human beings like you who need a home and safety and a future for our children?

How long will we stay refugees? Will we ever go home?

An Address to Human Beings

I am a leadbeater possum. I live in the Central Highlands of Victoria.

I know in your mind I'm only an animal, but actually I'm a lot like you. I struggle to raise my young to adulthood, to provide a home and safety so they can flourish. And like you and like the young family fleeing to Egypt in the story that you have just read, life can change quickly and I can find myself in danger, threatened with death not just for my young but for my whole extended family. Like you humans, I can be chased from my home and left without food, water or nesting holes. And what we have most in common is that our greatest predator is human beings. I've had to flee from my home several times when you bring in your big, noisy monsters to tear down our trees! Without them we have nowhere to nest and give birth, so we are dying out slowly and are now on the endangered list. But I guess that doesn't matter much to some of you.

I really feel sorry for you. What is it with you humans that makes you so greedy? Always wanting more land, more money, more power over others. You never seem to have enough! Your greed leads to poverty and suffering for many and you seem to think that's just how things are. As a species you still haven't grown up. So full of yourselves, you remain unaware or just thoughtless of your impact on others. You see creatures like me as something cute that amuses you, but without any sense that we are kin, related from the deep origins of the earth. Without this sense of kinship you see yourself as free to do as you please. You eat up the earth and spit it out as rubbish.

What chance have powerless creatures like me in a world where you control everything?

Will we always be on the run? Will we ever go home?

The chatter of two Inn-keepers... one of old, one of today...

Old: All these strangers coming into town! The place is overcrowded!

Today: Why don't they just go back to where they came from!

Old: Some say it's good for business but we're doing ok without them...

Today: They've come here from all over with their different ways and different lingo so the place doesn't feel like home anymore! Claiming to be refugees they say, but I bet they're just wanting to take our jobs and live a better life.

Old: There's just not enough room! I have to house people in the stable with the animals!

Today: Tent shanties are what they're making. The police should just come and clear them away. Who do these people think they are? Crossing borders at will and pushing themselves in like they have a right to be here!

Old: You watch... one day people will remember this influx...

Today: People need to get together and stop this happening! Who knows what will come of it!

Old: Yes, I was saying the same thing long ago and look what happened in Bethlehem!

Rachel Weeping

In this icon, we see Rachel seated in the midst of children, but looking closely we notice that the children's eyes are all closed in death. Rachel's arms are raised in loud lament and her voice reaches to the skies...

SCRIPTURE

Matthew 2:16-18

> When Herod saw that he had been tricked by the wise men, he was infuriated, and he sent and killed all the children in and around Bethlehem who were two years old or under, according to the time that he had learned from the wise men. Then was fulfilled what had been spoken through the prophet Jeremiah:
>
> > *A voice was heard in Ramah,*
> > *weeping and loud lamentation,*
> > *Rachel weeping for her children;*
> > *she refused to be consoled,*
> > *because they are no more.*

BACKGROUND

It is quite likely that this event did not actually happen historically. However, stories do not need to be historically correct in order to communicate something of the truth. This little vignette is situated during a time of Roman occupation and oppression. Herod, working in collusion with the Romans, is ruling with a heavy hand and creates conditions for this young family of Mary, Joseph and the infant Jesus, that cause them to flee to safety. Matthew, the Gospel writer, then quotes some verses from the prophet Jeremiah. Jeremiah was a prophet during the time of exile for the Jewish people and in chapter 31 he gives heart to the people by proclaiming that they will return to their land and their homes. He gives words of hope. It is interesting to note that when Matthew quotes Jeremiah, he takes only the image of Rachel weeping and omits the words of God speaking of hope for their future. We are left with a very poignant image...

This icon and Gospel passage invite us into the story of the destructive rage of a king who has been outwitted and in an attempt to hold his throne, orders the murder of "all the children in and around Bethlehem who were two years old or under..." There are echoes here of a former experience of loss centuries earlier when the descendents of Rachel were captured and deported. The grief of that experience is now joined with the grief of the mothers of Bethlehem as they face the death and destruction of their children.

This story is not just about an event a long time ago. It is so evocative that it brings before us all those mothers weeping for the senseless loss of their children in wars, in revenge attacks, in the acts of the powerful suppressing any threats to their position, in the imprisonment of political opponents, in the trafficking of human beings, in the industries that take their children into drug addiction or prostitution, in car accidents, in domestic violence, in the breakdown of relationships, in the countless acts of abuse that continue to harm the young and the not so young, throughout the world. The grief is not limited to the loss of physical life, but extends to the loss of life at all levels, the sense of self, of one's very worth.

In this brief quote from the Prophet Jeremiah that forms part of this small story, Rachel refuses to be consoled. She will not be beguiled by distraction or compromise. Her weeping and loud lamentation echoes down the centuries, calling us to maintain the rage that so naturally arises at the unthinkable death of children.

There is also a background echo here... We as human beings know so keenly the pain of losing children in death of any sort that we can stay stuck in our own grief and not notice that in the world around us many other mothers of different species are also weeping figuratively. Lamenting not only the death of their children, but in the process of extinction which so many of them are facing, they are lamenting the death of birth itself.

REFLECTION

Let us hear your voice, Rachel,
loud and shrill and unrelenting.
Let it hold the grief and tears
of women down the centuries
who have lost children
  to the bullet or the bomb,
  to cultural norms that define
    who is legitimate,
  to poverty and early death,
  to the scandal of extinctions,

to all those forces that suck life and hope
from the vulnerable.
Lament with loud cries, Rachel,
and do not cease.
Your rage is a force that transforms
that focuses
that empowers
to act and resist.
It engenders hope for a new future.
We join your voice, Rachel,
weeping...
loud
piercing
and unrelenting.

A voice from the other side...

The terror happened when we least expected it! It was night time when the weapons of powerful men were let loose. Bombs falling all around us, buildings collapsing in on top of whole families!

I was among the first of the dead. My ten years of life snuffed out in a second. From the other side, I could hear my mother wailing as she cradled me in her arms, holding me so tightly as if somehow she could breathe life back into my broken body. Soon her wailing was joined by so many others. How many lost their lives was never calculated. The 'enemy's' losses are never given the dignity of being counted, so we melt into oblivion."Collateral damage" is what they call it. Buildings, infrastructure, farms, crops, animals, human beings...All summed up in this one term!

Like the small children sacrificed at the hands of Herod long ago, our lives and deaths have no significance in the planning of powerful men. Their eyes are fixed on power, territory and the wealth that comes from it. Are they ever satisfied? As long as the answer is no, there will be no end to this devastation, no end to the weeping of mothers, even the land itself cries out for mercy, for an end...

Listening to the voice of the sky...

As the sky that surrounds the earth, I hear many things! People cry to the heavens in their distress, as if somehow their prayers will be heard up here!

Yes, there are trivial things that are asked...like to win the lottery (that's pretty common!) and then there are times when the prayer moves me to tears! The other day, for example, it was clear and bright, allowing the sun to shine softly on the earth when I overheard parliamentarians in several countries debating the necessity of turning boats away that were carrying refugees to their shores. At the very same moment, a boat had overturned in the Mediterranean Sea and a prayer came to my ears from a young mother, searching in vain for her infant who had been taken by the swirling water of the ocean, even as she herself struggled to stay afloat.

What world are human beings creating? Those living in comfort, making decisions about the lives of others so easily... Is compassion dead on the earth?

And the other day, there was the cry coming to me from the smallest of animals. Her habitat was being destroyed by bulldozers, there was no longer food for her and her offspring, nowhere to make a home to protect them. My heart went out to her as I knew already that no-one would listen to her cry and act to protect her. She was too small and insignificant in this new world... a world where human beings have lost their connection with and place on the Earth, where compassion that leads to action is seen as weakness and a threat to the comfort of the comfortable...

I hear all these cries. I hear best the cries of the vulnerable.

Earth weeps with Rachel...

As Rachel weeps for these children, so I weep for my own body that is being dismembered so brutally... the coral bleaching of the Great Barrier Reef, the destruction of the rainforests of the Amazon and Asia, the acidification of the oceans and the desertification of the land, the heating of the planet, the loss of countless species...is there no end to this brutality?

Can you not hear my groans as I suffer at your hands?

And you Christians... worst of all... you have had a past history of a close relationship with me and even today your leader, Francis, exhorts you to pay attention to my cries, to listen and act...

What will it take to wean you off such a greed for material things and for wealth? Until your grasp on these is loosened, there is no hope for me. And, in fact, there is no hope for you! For we flourish or perish together.

Sophia weeping

My name is Sophia/Wisdom and I am God's gift to humanity!
I have played with you from the time of your creation, delighting to be with you...
filling you with myself that you may act with wisdom.
How is it that now you do not let me in, shut me out, go your own way?
Where will I find human beings open to beauty... to goodness?
I weep that I may not find even one!

THE SAMARITAN WOMAN

In this icon, we see Jesus seated at the well. A woman from Samaria, the traditional enemies of the Jews, approaches him and enters into an extraordinary conversation. The background is mountainous, mountains being a symbol in icons for the place of revelation – the place of encounter with God.

SCRIPTURE

John 4:1-39

Now when Jesus learned that the Pharisees had heard 'Jesus is making and baptising more disciples than John – although it was not Jesus himself but his disciples who baptised – he left Judea and started back to Galilee. But he had to go through Samaria. So he came to a Samaritan city called Sychar, near the plot of ground that Jacob had given to his son Joseph. Jacob's well was there, and Jesus, tired out by his journey, was sitting by the well. It was about noon.

A Samaritan woman came to draw water, and Jesus said to her, 'Give me a drink'. His disciples had gone to the city to buy food. The Samaritan woman said to him, 'How is it that you, a Jew, ask a drink of me, a woman of Samaria?' (Jews do not share things in common with Samaritans.) Jesus answered her, 'If you knew the gift of God, and who it is that is saying to you, "Give me a drink", you would have asked him, and he would have given you living water'. The woman said to him, 'Sir, you have no bucket, and the well is deep. Where do you get that living water? Are you greater than our ancestor Jacob, who gave us the well, and with his sons and his flocks drank from it? Jesus said to her, 'Everyone who drinks of this water will be thirsty again, but those who drink of the water that I will give them will never be thirsty. The water that I will give will become in them a spring of water gushing up to eternal life.' The woman said to him, 'Sir, give me this water, so that I may never be thirsty, or have to keep coming here to draw water.'

Jesus said to her, 'Go, call your husband and come back.' The woman answered him, 'I have no husband.' Jesus said to her, 'You are right in saying "I have no husband"; for you have had five husbands, and the one you have now is not your husband. What you have said is true!' The woman said to him, 'Sir, I see that you are a prophet. Our ancestors worshipped on this mountain, but you say that the place where people must worship is in Jerusalem.' Jesus said to her, 'Woman, believe me, the hour is coming when you will worship the Father neither on this mountain nor in Jerusalem. You worship what you do not know; we worship what we know, for salvation is from the Jews. But the hour is coming, and is now here, when the true worshippers will worship the Father in Spirit and truth, for the Father seeks such as these to worship him. God is spirit, and those who worship him must worship in spirit and truth.' The woman said to him, 'I know that Messiah is coming' (who is called Christ). 'When he comes, he will proclaim all things to us.' Jesus said to her, 'I am he, the one who is speaking to you.'

Just then the disciples came. They were astonished that he was speaking with a woman, but no one said, 'What do you want? or Why are you speaking with her?'Then the woman left her water jar and went back to the city. She said to the people, 'Come and see a man who told me everything I have ever done! He cannot be the Messiah, can he? They left the city and were on their way to him...

Many Samaritans from that city believed in him because of the woman's testimony.

BACKGROUND

This is a powerful story, unique to John's Gospel. Whether it was an actual historical event or not, it was written into the Gospel in the light of the resurrection to validate the mission to the Samaritans and their inclusion among the disciples of Jesus. As such, it has a symbolic level of meaning that takes us beyond the literal face value of the story.

It seems that the community of John had a significant number of Samaritans who had come to believe in Jesus. This community came to understand that the things that formerly divided them such as their entrenched identities as Jew/Samaritan, as woman/man were no longer valid. That true worship, where one encounters God, is no longer where they thought it was– on this mountain or that – but now it takes place in the community of believers, among themselves.

This woman from Samaria is a central character in the story. She holds two places in the narrative, one as the individual woman engaged in a profound conversation with Jesus; and at the same time the Gospel writer makes her a figure of the wider community grappling with issues current to that community.

In the story it's midday. She goes to the well to draw water and there she meets Jesus. For readers in John's community, the mention of this detail would have evoked many other stories in their tradition where significant figures in their history met their wives/husbands at the well (for example Isaac and Rebekah, Jacob and Rachel, Moses and Zipporah). This also evokes the image of Jesus as Bridegroom, which the

Gospel writer uses elsewhere as well. So the reader becomes expectant... wondering... who's the bride? Remember... we are talking on a symbolic level here.

Jesus and this unnamed woman enter into a long and complex conversation. She questions him basically on every aspect of faith that causes division between the Jews and Samaritans. She speaks with great depth theologically and Jesus meets her every challenge.

At one point in their conversation, Jesus asks her about her husband, bringing to light the presence of 'five husbands'. This keeps the thread of tension around the 'bride and bridegroom' in the mind of the reader. It is possible that what is being referred to here are the five gods of neighbouring tribes who became mixed in with Samaritan worship. In the eyes of the Jews, this was infidelity to the God of Abraham, and here the evangelist presents Jesus as the Bridegroom wooing back the Samaritan community to fidelity to their relationship with God.

As a result of the woman's searching questions of Jesus, she not only comes to an experience of faith, but leaves what she was doing and goes to tell others about it. Her leaving her water jar behind echoes other Gospels where disciples were called in a similar way to leave their nets, boats, family, etc .to follow Jesus – a symbolic action indicating a call and a response to discipleship.

It is notable how such a strong biblical character – as this woman clearly is – is so easily diminished by centuries of preaching that insinuates she is a questionable character because of her supposed sexual engagement with five husbands. How easy it is to undermine a woman's authority and experience by calling her character into question by suggestions of sexual promiscuity. No similar ploy is used for male figures in traditional preaching. This has had a lasting impact on the teaching authority of women throughout the centuries and solidified the assumption that in the realm of 'the things of God' women are naturally inferior and should therefore hold a secondary position in relation to men.

The return of the male disciples in this story is an interesting interlude. Quite unnecessary to the overall story, their shock at returning and finding Jesus engaging with a woman is worth wondering about. They are uneasy when Jesus takes a woman seriously, particularly in an area they consider is their domain – in this case, the preaching of the Gospel.

Here is a woman succeeding in bringing others to faith. She does this on her own authority, because of her personal experience and conviction. She does not require the direction of men. One wonders if the inclusion of this seemingly unimportant narrative detail perhaps speaks to thorny issues currently alive and contentious in

John's community at the time. Were there strong women, preaching, teaching and leading in the community that posed a threat to the men who felt these activities were their domain by right of their being male? Was this causing tension in the community? Was the writer of this Gospel reclaiming the position of women as it was known in the lifetime of Jesus and shortly after his death – a position currently under attack at the time this Gospel was written?

REFLECTION

Water...

I'm in the centre of this story. Jesus comes to taste me and uses me as an image of the life that God desires for all created beings. All are called to taste this water of life. In fact I'm central to all your stories, for without me nothing lives. I have flowed through the Murray-Darling Basin for millennia, spreading life and abundance along my way long before human beings arrived. Today, however, I wonder if Jesus would use me as a symbol of abundant life... I am chocking with silt at the Coorong, ,and the lack of oxygen in some parts of me are causing enormous fish kills in the lower Darling at Menindee. Farmers and irrigators keep calling out for more allocations of water even as I struggle to breathe! Business, profits, and maintaining life as is rate far above my welfare. Who stops to really think what life will be like when I am dead? Will you keep carving me up even as I pass through my death throes? Does your compassion not extend this far?

Reflection from an outsider

They say we don't belong, that we are outsiders and shouldn't be making such a disturbance! What are we to do? We have come in to this community in the same way that they have, even though we aren't Jewish as they are. We are Samaritan, otherwise thought of as the Other... the enemy, somehow intrinsically different from them. They don't want us here. How do we come to such a position as humans... believing that there are some people who are 'in' and others who are 'out'? What a powerful position it is to be the ones who make this definition. It's age old and I can't see a change coming soon. But what does it do to us as human beings? It narrows our world and our heart. It also makes us very afraid of whoever this Other is because they become a constant threat, challenging our identity, our exclusiveness. And, of course, there is always fear that we'll take land, work and wealth.

But I am not a threat to them. I am a simple woman whose identity is being shaped as theirs is, by my coming to faith in this man Jesus. And I need to belong with others who share this experience too.

Being excluded is a cruel thing. Surely we human beings are better than this!

A conversation between Peter and Andrew

Peter: There he goes again! He's sitting there at the well with a woman! And talking with her! In full view! He never seems to worry what this looks like to others. I've spoken to him about this several times, but it doesn't make any difference. I'm older than him so you'd think he'd be respectful enough to listen to me!

Andrew: Pete, you've got a huge bee in your bonnet about this, haven't you? He sees things really differently from us. Being men in our culture, we're used to women being seen and treated as less than us, at least in public. But he relates to them as equals wherever he is. Not only that but he's interested in what they think and their opinions! He even searches it out!

Peter: That's what I mean! This disturbs me! If we start treating women really as our equals where will this take us? We'll have to listen to them, give them a real say in things and who knows what else! Andrew, this frightens me. I don't know how to be with that.

Andrew: Peter, you never change! You've always had to be the boss, the one everyone else refers to, even when you don't know what's going on! And now that we're involved in this movement with Jesus you're being taken into new territory. You don't like that. It unsettles you so you have to resist. I see it all the time in your relationship with Mary Magdalene, you're like a rock - immovable!

Peter: I don't know... I do like being in charge, even though I get things wrong at times. But what Jesus is asking of us in following him feels too damn hard. He keeps turning things on their head. I just don't get what he's on about!

Andrew: Yes, it is hard. But, you know, he has kept telling us that! Us blokes have certain things we have to learn or change. The women have their things too. But we can only do what is ours to do. None of us finds it easy, Peter. There are others like you too, who are digging their toes in and resisting. Equality isn't something we've been brought up with and it means we have to get off our perches a bit and make room for the women.

Peter: Yeah, I know he's right, but I'm not sure he knows what he's really doing. How long do you reckon it'll take for blokes like you and me to really get it and live differently, give over some of our power? I wager you, I won't see the day!

A female theologian reflects on bishops' concerns

Bishops: What are we to do with this woman theologian? She is questioning the traditional language we have used for God as though these words were put in the tradition by men and not by God!

Female theologian: I think we are coming from very different understandings of how Scripture and Tradition are formed. The human words we use when talking about God are not set in cement. God can't be contained by any limited words...so even words that have become sacrosanct like 'father' are always metaphorical. That is, they say something about what God is like, but they're not a definition because God can't be defined in our language. That's why we need lots of different words for God, the more the better since they expand our notion of God and remind us that God is always beyond any and all our words.

Bishops: She says that the all-male language used for God in the Tradition is "religiously inadequate" and perpetuates "an unequal relationship between women and men"! She doesn't understand that male images of God in scripture and tradition "are not mere human creations that can be replaced by others that we may find more suitable."

Female theologian: In so far as scripture conveys the word of God... is it not the case that biblical language, narratives and imagery communicate divine revelation? And if female images of God are part of that testimony...are they not legitimate witnesses of revelation? And is it not permitted that they form part of the repertoire of language about God within the community of faith? Is the church not permitted to use the language of Jesus when speaking about God?

(This imagined 'conversation' is based on the official statement by the Committee of Doctrine of the US Bishop's Conference 24 March 2011 and the response of female theologian Elizabeth Johnson 1 June 2011.)

THE DAUGHTER OF JAIRUS

The power of touch in healing.

SCRIPTURE

Mark 5:21-24, 35-43

> When Jesus had crossed again in the boat to the other side, a great crowd gathered round him; and he was by the sea. Then one of the leaders of the synagogue named Jairus came and, when he saw him, fell at his feet and begged him repeatedly, 'My little daughter is at the point of death. Come and lay your hands on her, so that she may be made well, and live.' So he went with him.
>
> And a large crowd followed him and pressed in on him...
>
> While he was still speaking, some people came from the leader's house to say, 'Your daughter is dead. Why trouble the teacher any further?' But overhearing what they said, Jesus said to the leader of the synagogue, 'Do not fear, only believe.' He allowed no one to follow him except Peter, James and John, the brother of James. When they came to the house of the leader of the synagogue, he saw a commotion, people weeping and wailing loudly. When he had entered, he said to them, 'Why do you make a commotion and weep? The child is not dead but sleeping.' And they laughed at him. Then he put them all outside, and took the child's father and mother and those who were with him, and went in where the child was. He took her by the hand and said to her, 'Talitha cum', which means, 'Little girl, get up!' And immediately the girl got up and began to walk about (she was twelve years of age). At this they were overcome with amazement. He strictly ordered them that no one should know this, and told them to give her something to eat.

BACKGROUND

This story forms a pair with the following story of the bleeding woman. It is constructed like a sandwich with the story of the bleeding woman forming the 'meat' and being wrapped around with this story of the daughter of Jairus.

The stories are also linked by both the gender of the ones healed and the issue of disease. The physicality of touch also has a prominent place in the narrative. Jesus doesn't just speak words of healing to her; he touches her, taking her by the hand and raising her to life. "Word and flesh on flesh together bring wholeness."[1]

The writer of this story mentions almost in passing that this girl is twelve years old. Some scholars read this as an indication that she is at or nearing the time of puberty, a very significant period of transition for a young woman. We do not know what this girl was suffering from, but there is a sense that it's a matter of life and death. The people around her believe the young girl is dying whereas Jesus says No, there is life here!

The verb that the writer of this story (Mark) uses to mean 'raise' is the same verb used when he talks about Jesus being raised from death. This story as it was listened to in the early church and as it continues to be heard in the community today, is received in a social context. In both periods, that cultural context is a gendered one. So proclaiming this story has a liberating message for women and men as they see this young woman being restored from apparent death to fullness of life.

REFLECTION

A letter from the daughter of Jairus to her grandmother

Dear Grandma,

I know you have been worried about me on hearing the news of my illness, so I am writing to put you at ease. This last bit of time has not been easy for me. No one told me that growing up would be so hard! I have felt lost for some time, behaving in ways that have made my parents sick with worry. That's a funny saying, isn't it? Like through worry I have shared my sickness with them!

Anyway, I have come through the hardest part and it's strange to say but I feel something has changed in me. I feel a new power in me to face my future and be able to meet whatever comes. I almost feel excited about it! Was it like this for you, Gran, when you were my age? Mum says we must thank God for getting me through this time. I don't know what God had to do with it, if anything. But I have experienced great care and kindness when I really didn't deserve it. Would that be like a trace of God, Gran? Is that how we experience her?

A 21st Century translation via sms

hi gran better now growing up hard talk soon xxxx

Grandmother's reply

My dearest Leah,

How happy and relieved I am to receive your letter. Yes, I have been worried about you for some time! Moving from childhood to adulthood is a tricky business, slow and sometimes dangerous. There were moments when your parents and I thought we had lost you as you got caught up in the wrong crowd. It was as though you had moved away from us and we felt powerless to know how to reach you. But I always had a sense that you would come through this troubled time.

Your mother tells you to thank God and I know that God has not figured much in your life till now. There are so many strange ideas about God these days, no wonder people want to throw God out! But you, Leah, already know this One we call God. You experienced her as you said in the kindness of others, even when you felt you may not have deserved it! God's face in the world is yours and mine and those who act with care and kindness. You have seen in your own experience how it brings you to life and gives you another chance when the odds are against you. As you continue on the road to adulthood, open yourself to this One who wants life for you and is closer to you than you can imagine. She will bring to fullness all the gifts she has bestowed on you… and they, my dear Leah, are many. I can't wait to see you grow and blossom in all directions! Love to your Mum and Dad and a special hug to you. Come and visit me soon.

Gran xx

A 21st Century translation via sms

Hi sweetie! you're spot on to give thanks! Love you!

Gran. Xx

The Bleeding Woman

A vulnerable woman in a male world, this icon brings us into relationship with her as she searches for healing and hope.

SCRIPTURE

Mark 5:25-34

> Now there was a woman who had been suffering from haemorrhages for twelve years. She had endured much under many physicians, and had spent all that she had; and she was no better, but rather grew worse. She had heard about Jesus, and came up behind him in the crowd and touched his cloak, for she said, ' If I but touch his clothes, I will be made well.' Immediately her haemorrhage stopped; and she felt in her body that she was healed of her disease. Immediately aware that power had gone forth from him, Jesus turned about in the crowd and said, 'Who touched my clothes?' And his disciples said to him, 'You see the crowd pressing in on you; how can you say, "Who touched me?"' He looked all around to see who had done it. But the woman, knowing what had happened to her, came in fear and trembling, fell down before him and told him the whole truth. He said to her, ' Daughter, your faith has made you well; go in peace, and be healed of your disease.'

BACKGROUND

This story is linked with the raising of Jairus' daughter. It is a story of a woman who at some stage may have had some wealth and status (5:26) but now is desperate at many levels. In an ancient cultural context, it is extraordinary that she is in a public place on her own with no male protector and that she would dare to touch a strange male without his consent–violating the modesty code for women. One also notices that she is not identified, either by a personal name or in relationship to a male. Is she married? Does she have children?

Elaine Wainwright seems to imply that women who were bleeding either due to menstruation or other illnesses were not excluded from their homes and family, even though there were restrictions on them and on those around them.

The woman's action is quite audacious in that she takes the initiative in her own healing and in doing so she violates both the social and religious codes of her time. There is no story in the New Testament where any woman asks Jesus for a miracle for herself. Either others ask for her or Jesus takes the initiative himself. It is also noteworthy that this woman had the power to draw healing power from Jesus without him choosing to do so beforehand.

The disciples question Jesus about the futility of his enquiry regarding who touched him in the midst of the crowd. This alerts us to something important. The woman's touch was one of faith – an action very different from the accidental jostling of the crowd.

This is the first time that the Gospel of Mark shows Jesus and a woman conversing one on one.[1] Jesus is drawn into the world of women through his own insistence on meeting the one who had drawn power from him. As in the related story of the daughter of Jairus and the story of the mother-in-law of Peter, touch is a significant thread running through each. Touch is a powerful form of communication. It has social, psychological and even healing properties. It has symbolic meaning and invites reciprocity. When two living creatures touch, there is the possibility of a crossing over, an entering into the world of the other. This can happen between all sorts of people and as well between humans and other-than-human creatures. In this particular story, it is Jesus who crosses over into the marginal world of this bleeding woman.

Something else to keep in mind when reading this story... Mark uses an expression when describing her. He says that 'she suffered much'. Later in Mark's Gospel, he uses this expression twice to describe the suffering and death by crucifixion awaiting Jesus as he pursues his healing work. It is as though in her own body this woman carries symbolically what awaits Jesus the healer.

> *"She carries suffering in her body as Jesus did and she both desires and effects healing in her body symbolising in a quite extraordinary way the healing power of Jesus, power that he was not prepared to use on his own account."* [2]

Jesus responds to the woman with the words, 'Daughter, your faith has made you well..' Faith in this instance has several components. It involves a belief that Jesus has the power to actually heal her physically, and the courage to take initiative based on this belief, to reach out and touch him, even when it involves breaking cultural rules. This faith has the capacity to empower the disempowered, to bring life and wholeness. Her story is one both of her own transformation, but also for the reader of Mark's community as for the reader of today; she alerts us to the transformation inherent in a life of discipleship and encourages us to pursue it.

Elaine Wainwright directs our attention to this transformation when she says:

> *"The materiality of touch, of bodies, of skin with its attendant crossing-over reminds us that touching in this story takes place on the margins. It invites*

readers to cross over into another space in which the human and other-than-human can touch and be touched in a way that makes for wholeness and transformation in these relationships also. It is to this end that the story of the woman with the haemorrhage invites contemporary readers seeking feminist, ecological and post-colonial transformation." [3]

REFLECTION

Blood, rich red, holding life
but for me
a consignment to a half-life
straining family relationships
unable to pray with my sisters
life is lonely, desperate.

What have I to lose?
I am beyond social judgment
Let me take this chance
be bold!

there... I have touched his garment...
I can feel a change in my body
this healing makes me whole and clean again!
but my touch has made him impure now
and until evening he will wear my burden.
He has noticed my touch,
so different from that of the noisy crowd
come to see this miracle worker
hungry for a show, a spectacle.
He calls out to find who has touched him
in this way.
So used to feeling shame I come forward cringing
waiting for the reprimand that is sure to come
but no censure here
he calls me 'daughter'

no abusive names for one
who dares step out from proper behaviour
but a word that gives me relationship again
respect and honour.
The healing he gives goes further than my illness
it touches my whole being
freeing me from fear that has held me bound
restoring me to life and love
and community
giving all a new hope and a future.

Hannah's Story

My name is Hannah. I was on the street yesterday, on my way to meet my friend Ruth. We were going to play with some of our friends from the other end of town. On my way I passed a crowd in the street, jostling and calling out to this man. I could just see his head in the crowd and had to struggle not to get caught in the crush of the forward movement. He seemed to have a certain authority in his person. He stopped suddenly and asked who touched him. A strange question in the face of the crowd pressing around him! I froze, expecting some reprimand to come from him and have someone dragged in front to receive it! I kept to the side, not wanting to get caught in something ugly. But then what I saw was amazing.

This woman came forward. She had been crouching down within the crowd so as not to be seen. She clearly was not well and had a look of someone who had suffered a lot. A woman alone in a crowd of men. She was so brave! She spoke up and told everyone that she had touched this man hoping to be cured from her ailment. I held my breath. I couldn't take my eyes off her. There was something about her, a gutsiness even in face of her weakness.

This man listened to her carefully. He called her 'daughter' and gave her what she wanted! I watched her as the crowd continued on their way. She stood up straight. The power and life she exuded was palpable. She turned around and walked on her way with an air of self- confidence that stunned me! My eyes followed her until she disappeared into the distance. Something extraordinary had happened here and I was spellbound!

Daughter...

'DAUGHTER' he called me! So now I have a new father! Once again I'm under a male! Now that I'm accepted back into my religious and social family group, I have to take up once again the traditional role of a woman! I am seen as either a source of shame or honour, so I have to be careful of my behaviour, conform to cultural norms.

This healer has spoken before about establishing a new type of family not based on ties of blood but on our relationship with God, a new sort of family where everyone is equal. Funny that... even as he healed me he returned me to that old form of family where women have to know their place. A double-sided gift! I wonder if he realised?

The Widow of Nain

A widow's grief moves the heart of God.

SCRIPTURE

Luke 7:11-17

Soon afterwards he went to a town called Nain, and his disciples and a large crowd went with him. As he approached the gate of the town, a man who had died was being carried out. He was his mother's only son, and she was a widow; and with her was a large crowd from the town.

When the Lord saw her, he had compassion for her and said to her, 'Do not weep.' Then he came forward and touched the bier, and the bearers stood still. And he said, 'Young man I say to you, rise!' The dead man sat up and began to speak, and Jesus gave him to his mother.

Fear seized all of them; and they glorified God saying, 'A great prophet has risen among us!' and 'God has looked favourably on his people!' This word about him spread throughout Judea and all the surrounding country.

BACKGROUND

This story is unique to Luke and it gives us an insight into the depth of feeling Jesus has for those who suffer.

Luke portrays Jesus as the benefactor of widows. For those hearing the story, it would have reminded them of how God takes on the role as the defender of widows in the Jewish scriptures e.g. Psalm 68 refers to God as "A father of the fatherless, a defender of widows is God in his holy habitation."

As we have seen in other 'widow' stories, women who had lost a husband were often reduced to poverty and could be quite vulnerable within the society. Here is a woman who has not only been widowed but now has lost her only son.

In this story, a silent, mourning woman who has lost her place in society and has been reduced to dependency or poverty, moves Jesus to act on her behalf and restore her son. While one may see in this story a minimising of this woman's experience as she remains voiceless and nothing further is said of her. Barbara Reid offers another interpretation when she says, "... she prompts Jesus to take up the cause of one who is voiceless."[1] It is the eloquence of her silence and tears that impacts on Jesus. He is deeply moved in a way that some commentators describe as 'gut-wrenching'. Does it remind him of his own mother who also may have been a widow?

And if Jesus is the face of God... what does this story tell us about God?

The story calls to mind those mothers throughout the world whose silent protest at the death or disappearance of their loved ones continues to this day e.g. the Madres de la Plaza de Mayo of Argentina following the 'dirty war' of the 1970s.

Another way of listening to this story is to recall the story of the burning bush from Exodus 3:1-12. The Israelites are suffering in slavery in Egypt and God speaks to Moses..."I have seen the misery of my people... I have **heard** their cry... I **know** well what they are suffering...Therefore I **have come down** to **deliver** them..."

The Holy One is not distant from the suffering of the people but is deeply involved with those in distress. With this reminder of Moses' encounter with God from Hebrew Scriptures as a background, the scene of Jesus' response to the widow evokes powerfully the God he had come to know and shares with us.

And once hearing of the compassion of God and seeing it in action in the life and work of Jesus, we are left with both a personal and communal challenge...

> *"God is not only to be contemplated but also to be practised. If the heart of divine mystery is turned in compassion toward the world, then devotion to this God draws persons into the shape of divine communion with all others: Be merciful, just as your Father is merciful."* [2]

REFLECTION

A widow muses

Kindness is a funny word... a bit out of fashion these days... but how powerful it can be when it touches us! I've never thought about it much before now. It always seemed to me to be something optional... if I felt like it... You see, I've always been in the position of giving it but my son's death put me in a very different place! The ache of loss and grief was overwhelming to say nothing of the social and economic position it left me in!

My life was changed and I was spinning, lost in a world of unreality, when a stranger passed and, without being asked, acted with kindness towards me and my son with such generosity and freedom! How could I ever forget?

The power of such kindness has changed me beyond anything I could imagine! It's like... it's like I met God in this man.... but how can that be?

Death

Here I am again; doing my job as usual and along comes this guy and undoes it all!! What to do??

Kindness

They call me a virtue! That doesn't sit comfortably with me. In reality, I'm pretty ordinary, just a basic human value. Actually, I'm from a large family. Some of my sisters and brothers are thoughtfulness, appreciation, patience, self-giving...

Our job is to bring people to life from the inside. Like with this woman and her son, we can actually raise the dead... metaphorically speaking, that is!!

We're available to all human beings but we are a bit bashful... we need to be chosen, to be invited. We're rather averse to pushiness...

But when you let us in... Wow! Do we have a good time! Things come to life all around us, even from the most unexpected places...

THE CALL OF THE MOTHER-IN-LAW OF PETER

In this icon of the healing of the mother-in-law of Peter we are invited into relationship with her and into the power of human touch to bring about healing... and more.

SCRIPTURE

Matthew 8:14-15

> When Jesus entered Peter's house, he saw his mother-in-law lying in bed with a fever; he touched her hand, and the fever left her, and she got up and began to serve him.

BACKGROUND

How can we read this short story?

The woman 'serves' (*diakonia*) Jesus in this story, not everyone. The word diakonia is a multi-meaning word. It ranges from the daily domestic work of women and slaves to public roles in the service of the state. Among early Christians it held the meaning of domestic service but also that of the service of discipleship and ministry as they developed practices of hospitality and liturgical expression within the community. Some Scripture scholars see in this story a call to discipleship and the traces of the community's memory of Peter's mother-in-law and of her ministry within the community.

Jesus enters into the presence of a woman lying sick. This action breaches the usual norms of public/private space. Elaine Wainwright[1] describes it as a 'borderland' story, on the border of both gender and cultural norms regarding space. In this particular story, boundaries are being redefined with regard to women and social convention. Jesus takes the initiative in this healing story which is unusual in gospel accounts of healing. This puts him on the border again, stretching the boundaries of what is culturally acceptable for his time.

What is the sickness that this woman is suffering from? She is laid low, unable to resume her normal household duties, even that of hospitality with the arrival of Jesus. Scripture stories are rich and can be read with different levels of meaning. Could we hear in this story the weight of expectations borne by women with their cultural and physical demands... enough to send the mother-in-law of Peter into a fever and leave her incapacitated? Could it be a reference to the opposition women experienced to their being followers of Jesus, to their being full and equal members of the community forming around Jesus during his lifetime and after? We can wonder.

Jesus touches her and it is this touch that brings about healing. He uses the power of ordinary human touch as the vehicle for healing and transformation. The verb used here by Matthew has the same connotation as that used in describing the raising of Jesus from the dead, that is, being brought to a whole new form of life And the service the mother-in-law of Peter renders is not a single event but an ongoing activity, taking her model of service from Jesus' life and teaching. Since Jesus devoted his life to serving those who were subjugated and oppressed in society so that they may come to wholeness, this then would have been the model for the mother-in-law of Peter. When Jesus taught his disciples what it means to be his disciples, he made it clear that he himself stood at the opposite extreme from those with power who only asked to be served.

As Elaine Wainwright notes[2] In the ongoing activity of diakonia, the mother-in-law of Peter continues, beyond the healing transformation, to carry in her body the having-been-raised-ness of Jesus and her response to this healing is to 'serve' in the same way as Jesus.

Reading this story as a call to discipleship – to the following of a way of being in the world that Jesus both spoke about and lived, one that gave women equal status in the life of the newly forming community where the hallmarks are mutual service based on love, equity and compassion – offers readers of today a new insight into the life and ministry of women in the early Jesus movement. It also offers hope for women's engagement now and into the future.

REFLECTION

A conversation between Peter and his mother-in-law (let's call her Naomi)

Naomi: I've learnt something today Peter. Something about family that I have missed till now.

Peter: There's not much that you miss around here!

Naomi: I've been unsettled since your friend left us today. He showed us a way of being that I find quite attractive.

Peter: What do you mean? He calmed your fever and helped you to your feet but I didn't notice anything other than that!

Naomi: There is something about how he relates that is quite different. Firstly, as soon as he entered our house, he came directly to me.

Peter: He probably noticed you were not there to offer hospitality.

Naomi: Yes, so he came looking for me! He didn't have to do that. He didn't stand on ceremony or worry about custom or what people would say. He came right over and touched me! Yes, the fever did leave me, but there was something more remarkable than that. I can't get the experience out of my mind. It has made me remember the story of Moses and the burning bush where God says to Moses, 'I have seen the misery of my people who are in Egypt, I have heard their cry, I know their suffering, and I have come down to deliver them...' God sees when we suffer and is moved, moved deeply enough to act. Now, there was something of that experience of God that I tasted in this man. It's like I hear in him an echo of what God is like!

Peter: Have you still got a touch of fever?

Naomi: No, he cured my fever, but something has changed in me, Peter. The fever has gone but there is something else in its place! It's like a new zest for life, a hunger for this God he talks about, this one who has the compassion of a mother, who creates a family of equals, a sense of kinship that doesn't have the usual boundaries, who is closer to us than the air we breathe! I tell you, Peter, this changes everything!

Peter's mother-in-law reflects as she reads Matthew's Gospel

I am an old woman now... much has happened since my first encounter with the One known as Jesus...

I have in my hand a piece of writing that people are calling the Gospel according to Matthew... it makes an interesting read and the community is quite excited about it. However, there is an unsettledness within me and I'm pondering what it is that leaves me on edge...

I'm left wondering what sort of God is being projected here. Does it ring true with what we have experienced in our time with Jesus? What expectations of women and men does it hold and how do these affect the lives of women and girls in this movement? And men too, I guess!

My fear is really about how will it be interpreted and preached. Already there is a strong tendency to focus on 'The Twelve' as though these are the leaders and notice that 'The Twelve' doesn't include any of the women who were followers of Jesus and have been leading local communities very successfully. If you just listened to the language, you couldn't be blamed for thinking that all human beings are male and to be female is some lesser form of creature. And while this story of my encounter with Jesus is included, it has been taken up in preaching as a simple healing story that ends in placing me once again in the traditional women's role of performing household tasks. Nothing is said about the mission I held in this early movement of the followers of Jesus.

Jesus was very clear about having women on an equal footing with men in the community and this caused friction alright. It was going against custom and long held beliefs about women being inferior. But he was uncompromising! And now, since his death, there is a turning back to the old ways as though this issue isn't as important as other more pressing ones... at least in the view of our male leaders! I'm afraid for my daughters and granddaughters. What will the future hold for them in this community? Will they be relegated once again to second class members, to being the servant or helper of male leaders, while their own gifts and capacities for leadership are left undeveloped and ignored? And will this situation then be sanctified by it being written into this Gospel and read as the word of God! It's a slippery slope... wish I could see what his group would be like in 500 years' time!

Peter's wife remembers...

I remember the day as clear as anything! My mother was sick, quite unusual for her, and sick enough to send her to bed. Jesus arrived with Peter, my husband. Mum was anxious as hospitality was a big thing with her and she did not want to be neglectful of this visitor. But there was nothing to be done as her illness had laid her low.

This Jesus was an interesting character. Peter had been spending a lot of time with him and, to be honest, it was annoying me somewhat! Whenever I needed him for something, he was gone! Anyway on that day this teacher turned the customs of hospitality on their head and went over to her to see how she was. Not content with offering simple, get well wishes, he reached out towards her and healed her! In an instant she was up and at it! But I noticed a change in her that went way beyond a bodily healing. She became attentive to this teacher and began conforming her life to the things he was both preaching and living. In fact, she became his disciple. Peter had mixed feelings about this but I could see her coming to life in a whole new way, so I encouraged her and defended her against criticism. She became tireless in her work for this community forming around Jesus and worked hard for years after Jesus' death.

This was the day that changed everything for her and, after all this time, I remember it well!

Sophia Wisdom...

I've been listening to Peter's mother-in-law... she's worried about the male take-over of the community and the struggle women are having in remaining as equals as Jesus had practised. I've been listening to this struggle and the complaints of women for 2000 years. Not much has changed. She was right to be worried!

Story of Martha and Mary

In this icon, we have a rather traditional image with Jesus seated and holding a scroll representing the Word of God, Martha having a word with him and Mary sitting in a docile manner at his feet. There has been one small but significant change – Martha is not carrying something from the kitchen, but rather a copy of the Gospels. Let's see what makes this significant...

SCRIPTURE

Luke 10:38-42

> Now as they went on their way, Jesus entered a certain village, where a woman named Martha welcomed him into her home. She had a sister named Mary, who sat at the Lord's feet and listened to what he was saying. But Martha was distracted by her many tasks; so she came to him and asked. 'Lord, do you not care that my sister has left me to do all the work by myself? Tell her then to help me.' But the Lord answered her, 'Martha, Martha, you are worried and distracted by many things; there is need of only one thing. Mary has chosen the better part, which will not be taken away from her'.

BACKGROUND

It often happens that when women read this story, there's a certain discomfort – one that usually isn't raised clearly, if at all. How can one disagree with Jesus!? And it's this very bind that is a clue to understanding what's being communicated in this story. In the introduction, we mentioned the need for feminist readers – both women and men – to be suspicious especially when there seems to be a ruling with regard to women... So let's be suspicious.

In this story, Martha who is feisty and has a voice is rebuffed while Mary who chooses the place of a subordinate student is praised. Jesus is placed in the centre of the story (in patriarchy the Master has a central place). Mary who sits at the Master's feet as the silent woman is approved of, while Martha who argues on her own behalf is silenced. And just as Martha's voice is taken away, so too Mary remains without her own voice. Sister is put up against sister. Both are forced to conform to patriarchal norms.

First, against the general assumption in much preaching, there is no mention of Martha being in the kitchen. She complains about being left to do all the work and the word used in the text is *diakonia*, which is used for a variety of forms of ministerial service within the community including hospitality, financial support and the ministry of the table and of the word. As the community developed over time, this term became a more technical term that referred to eucharistic table service, proclamation and ecclesial leadership. According to Barbara Reid, Martha's complaint isn't that Mary has left her to do the service of hospitality but rather that Mary has been persuaded to sit silently at the feet of Jesus and leave the more public ministries such as preaching, leading liturgical rituals in house-churches and possibly baptising, to the men.[1] Eventually, the *diakonia* of women was subordinated to that of men so that in the Acts of the Apostles (sequel to the Gospel of Luke) there is no mention of the *diakonia* of women, but only that of men. Luke would have known that both men and women were engaged in spreading the good news of Jesus so why repress it? What point is being made? And who is making it?

The use of the term 'Lord' to address Jesus is a clue that this story was formed after the resurrection of Jesus and may not have been an actual historical event. Rather, it has been crafted within a community wrestling with the 'problem' of women's public ministry. The need to put such a firm response on the lips of Jesus suggests that something was already happening in terms of women taking their own authority to speak publicly about God even when their experience differed and possibly contradicted the official line that was being developed at the end of the first century of the Christian era. Women claiming their public voice has always been problematic... and even more so when they claim to know something of the living God.

In *But She Said*, Elizabeth Schussler Fiorenza sees this story as pitting the women of the Jesus movement who were acting in apostolic ministries against each other. It uses the words put into the mouth of Jesus as a way of restricting the ministry and authority of women. She sees the gospel writer taking sides and enlisting Jesus to silence women leaders in the house-churches who were speaking up and protesting; and at the same time praising the silent and subordinate behaviour of Mary.

So, as Fiorenza exhorts us...let us be clear: it is the gospel writer Luke and not the risen Jesus who supports and promulgates such restrictions on women. What we are reading is not the Word of God, but the word of Luke.[2]

How then do we hear this story in the 21st century?

Reading it 'against the grain' allows us to step back from the centuries of preaching and hear this story as a prescription that stifles women's struggle against the growing patriarchal culture of the church at that time. It allows us to say 'No' to a dualistic framework and to reclaim the voice of both these women, together with their authority to speak theologically; to have their voices heard and validated. And more importantly for women today it encourages us to claim our own relationship with God, explore it and talk about it publicly without waiting for clerical permission and in fact we are – in homes, in 'market places' and in the written word. And, of equal importance, it encourages women to claim their rightful place within the community as fully baptised members and so eligible for roles of leadership and service, equal to male members.

The patriarchal culture of the Church remains engrained today, long after this story was first told. So the discomfort that women have often felt when listening to it needs to remain sharp with an edge that shapes our response to the silencing and subordinating of women in our world, in any shape or form, with a practical commitment to solidarity and justice.

REFLECTION

An alternative version of Luke 10:38-42

Now as they went on their way, Jesus entered a certain village, where a woman named Martha welcomed him into her home. She had a sister named Mary, who sat at the Lord's feet and listened to what he was saying. The apostles also were there and a discussion began. Peter spoke up and said, 'Lord, we have a problem. Martha has been out preaching with us and it's causing trouble among our followers.'

'What's the problem, Peter?' asked Jesus. Peter replied,'People are saying that the women among us don't know their place; their appearance in public alongside of us goes against all our cultural and religious customs; and they're afraid that women may lose a sense of their proper place in our community. Our tradition has always valued women and their contribution in the home, but public preaching like Martha has been doing is going too far.'

Martha then spoke up. 'Lord, the men among us are encouraging women to stay at home, not to be in public and certainly not to speak of our experiences of faith. They say we should learn from our husbands at home and that should be enough for us. Mary has been listening to them. She is still young and impressionable... but I know her. Both of us, and others too, have a fire inside – its warmth and light will burst from us, whatever the men say.

'It is you who have lit this flame in us – will you see it quenched?'

Conversation between Mary and Martha

Mary: What do you think about this story written about us in the Gospel?

Martha: Well, I didn't like being silenced! It's hard enough for us women to have a voice in the first place let alone to be heard and taken seriously! Using a story where I get silenced... and by Jesus... just doesn't give a good message to other women.

Mary: I agree! You didn't get heard, did you? And pitting us against each other didn't go down well with me either! Like the way you are in the world is not quite ok, but my way is! There's no place for difference here.

Martha: Difference is a tricky thing! We don't deal with it very well and this story encourages us to take sides and to hear that there are only two options, one good and one bad. And it gives value to one way only by disparaging the other.

Mary: And it is set up in such a way that the 'right' option will maintain the status quo with regard to women's position, what we can do and can't do according to the male leaders.

Martha: That's spot on, Mary. And sometimes it's other women who hold these restrictive views too and really push them! If I was writing this story, I'd have Jesus say...

"Yes, Martha, there is much to do in the service of the community and many hands and feet are needed! Social restrictions are placed on you as a woman, Martha. And there is much pressure to conform, but I say to you... and to your sister Mary too... don't stop speaking and working in whatever ways suit you. You are made in the image of God, just as your brother is. Hold on to that and don't stop giving the service that is yours to give regardless of what others say or how they try to curb your engagement."

Mary: Without being offensive to Luke who wrote this story, I think it would have been better if a woman had written it!

Martha: Possibly... she would have had to be brave because if she was honest, and spoke about the issue that was behind this story, she'd get a bit of flack. It's interesting how whenever women raise the issue of their exclusion, it just seems to invite argument. It's just so hard to be really heard. I never had that problem with Jesus though. He really understood and didn't need to be defensive whenever there was an issue of women being equal to men. Gender didn't seem to be an issue with him at all!

Mary's friend Salome expresses her frustration...

How do you make a woman see clearly! Mary is so happy to sit at the feet of the teacher in silence, as though she is a disciple or a student! But that's just being a sponge! To be a disciple means asking questions, engaging in dialogue, grappling with the teacher and his teaching. But she sits there in silence! No, this isn't being a disciple, it's just being an audience.... and even a chook can do that! Who knows what she picks up as she sits there. It remains private, unshared and so does not build up the community! There is more to her than that, but how do I get her to see?

MARTHA PROFESSES HER FAITH

Martha engages with Jesus in a profound conversation about life and death.

SCRIPTURE

John 11:1-6; 17-27

> Now a certain man was ill, Lazarus of Bethany, the village of Mary and her sister Martha. Mary was the one who anointed the Lord with perfume and wiped his feet with her hair; her brother Lazarus was ill. So the sisters sent a message to Jesus, 'Lord, he who you love is ill.' But when Jesus heard it, he said, 'This illness does not lead to death; rather it is for God's glory, so that the Son of God may be glorified through it'. Accordingly, though Jesus loved Martha and her sister and Lazarus, after having heard that Lazarus was ill, he stayed two days longer in the place where he was...
>
> When Jesus arrived, he found that Lazarus had already been in the tomb for four days. Now Bethany was near Jerusalem, some two miles away, and many of the Jews had come to Martha and Mary to console them about their brother. When Martha heard that Jesus was coming, she went and met him, while Mary stayed at home. Martha said to Jesus, 'Lord, if you had been here, my brother would not have died. But even now I know that God will give you whatever you ask of him.' Jesus said to her, 'Your brother will rise again.' Martha said to him, 'I know that he will rise again in the resurrection on the last day'. Jesus said to her, 'I am the resurrection and the life. Those who believe in me, even though they die, will live, and everyone who lives and believes in me will never die. Do you believe this?' She said to him, 'Yes, Lord, I believe that you are the Messiah, the Son of God, the one coming into the world.'

BACKGROUND

In this story, we meet Martha and Mary again, but in a very different context! The writer of John's Gospel introduces them to us not as sisters in tension but rather as close friends of Jesus... 'Jesus loved Martha and her sister and Lazarus'. Naming Martha first among the group gives her a certain prominence and within the story we see that she has a clear voice and uses it, rather than being silenced as in Luke's story.

The setting of the encounter between Jesus and Martha is within a wider one, commonly known as the raising of Lazarus. While the story climaxes in the raising of Lazarus, the heart of this story is the conversation between Martha and Jesus. This episode reveals a faith community grappling with the question of death.[1] How is it that as followers of Jesus they believe in eternal life and yet still have to face death? How do they respond to those around them who challenge them on this issue?

Martha, then, becomes the representative of the community that is left behind. It is in this context that the conversation between Martha and Jesus takes place.

Martha voices the belief of the community when she says that if Jesus had been there, then Lazarus would not have died – meaning that Jesus is expected to do something to remove the scandal of death which the community is really struggling with. Jesus meets Martha's expectation with a challenge... does she believe in him and what he has come to reveal about the bounty of God? That the eternal life God gives us does not do away with physical death but transcends it? This is a significant leap of faith both for Martha and for the community as it is for us today. The writer of this Gospel then has Jesus offer her the invitation to faith... 'Do you believe this?'

Jesus' question offers her (and the believing community) a challenge to go beyond their traditional forms of belief and be open to the radical fullness of life that he is offering.

Martha gets it and responds positively to the offering.

Her response parallels Peter's profession of faith in Matthew's Gospel, a passage often used to confirm Peter's leadership in the community. Sandra Schneiders remarks, concerning John's story:

> *"The representative role of Martha is difficult to understand unless women in John's community actually did function as community leaders. But whatever role women held in the Johannine community, the Gospel text as it stands presents Jesus as addressing the foundational question to a woman and the woman as responding, on her own responsibility, with the Christian confession of faith. If this confession, given during the public life of Jesus, grounds the promise of the primacy to Peter, it is no less significant as foundation of community leadership when given by a woman."* [2]

Martha moves from a position of wanting Jesus to take death away to a deeper theological position as she converses with him. As a representative figure, she voices the coming to faith of the community as she says: ' Yes, Lord, I believe...'

In this story, the Gospel writer known as John shifts a miracle story about the raising of Lazarus to a story about the fullness of life that is offered to all who come to faith in Jesus.

REFLECTION

Martha addresses the reader

Have you ever felt the sting of death, the loss of one you love? It creates an aching hollow deep inside and threatens to swallow you up. Even though over time the pain eases, it always threatens to raise its head at an unexpected moment and knock you around.

Lazarus, Mary and I were always very close even in spite of our different personalities. When Lazarus died unexpectedly, it was like my world just collapsed. I had been a friend and follower of Jesus and heard about his promise of eternal life, but I was facing something that gave the lie to all this religious talk. I had no words for the terrible ache and void that was engulfing me and a promise of something in the distant future had no meaning for me, it was too unreal. So when Jesus turned up (two days late!), I just didn't want to hear this pie in the sky stuff! I wanted to challenge him. How could this God he talked about so often allow all human beings, and maybe animals too, to suffer such grief as a 'normal' part of life? He had no answer to my particular question, but turned my challenge around onto me. Could I believe that there is an existence, a presence beyond death? That we don't just disappear into nothing? Dare I believe that God's love accompanies us through the process of death and into something else beyond what we know or can conceive? That God never abandons us even in the face of something as incomprehensible as death?

I'm a pretty rational, practical sort of woman, so this was really stretching me. There was nothing I could see that would prove what he was saying. I had come to know him as a trustworthy person, one whose sense of the real and of how things worked in life was probably more acute than my own, but that in itself was not enough for me to just swallow what he was saying. He had asked me directly if I believed this, but I couldn't answer him immediately, even though the gospel story gives the impression I had an answer on the tip of my tongue just waiting to leap out! In fact, I sat with it for sometime. In the end, I asked myself what difference does it make if I believe or not? If what he is saying is real, it will be so whether I believe or not! And if it's not true and I was taken in, would I lose much?

If, on the other hand, I was to make the leap and take this belief on, it would open to me the possibility of some sort of on-going relationship with Lazarus in the here and now, even though it would be so different from what we had known. It would ease some of the sting of his physical absence. And it would help me take up my life again with a sense of hope. And I have learnt the power of hope, even the finest sliver of it!

As I pondered all this, I came to realise that what was being asked of me was not a yes/no answer to life after death, but something else altogether. I was being invited into a deepening relationship with this God of Jesus, a relationship – not an acceptance of a set of 'facts'. As in any relationship, it required of me a leap into the dark. Could I make it? Could I trust this One we call God?

I sat with him later and as we talked, I could see that it was really all about love! The love this God has for us and for everything. A love that invites us in, gently, patiently and when we allow ourselves to be drawn in we already taste what this 'eternal life ' is now, in the present. So when we pass through death, it is this love that does not end and holds us in existence beyond our physical demise.

Real love is not irrational, but it does take us to a different place. Finding myself in this place, there was a quiet sense of knowing. Not scholarly knowing based on proofs, something different but no less solid, no less open to ongoing questions and wonderings. No words could capture my response to him, only a readiness for relationship and where it would take me!

The regent honeyeater has a word to say...

I'm taken aback by all this talk about life after death! I'm just wanting life before death! I'm on the endangered list and hope for my survival and that of my species is looking pretty grim. I want to live and I want my young to live after me. None of this theological and philosophical talk for me! While you spend time on such musings, I'm dying... worse still... going into extinction!

You Christians talk about a God who is gracious and merciful, so when are you going to act like this One? You might pray for our Earth, its creatures and our struggle as we cry out, but don't you realise that God cannot hear unless you, the people, listen and act? God doesn't have any hands, except yours... and that goes for voice and power to act. So get cracking!!

Gabriel is back again...!

Here I am again... Gabriel the archangel... (not quite sure what the arch is about, but yes, I'm an angel). You met me earlier at the Annunciation. I do get around a bit! I've just been listening to Martha and the regent honeyeater and their musings on death and life... I can't resist! I want to put in my tuppence worth too!

Imagination is the word!

We need lots of it. It tends to get a bad rap as though it is just about fairytale stuff, but the world as we know it would not be as it is today without human beings having heaps of imagination and using it! The scientists, explorers, mathematicians, writers, artists... they all would have used their imaginations and it helped them see what was as yet unseen, unknown... and for some, unimaginable! And once imagined, they could work towards it, whatever it was.

So when we come to issues of life and death, you humans need to draw on your imaginations in the same way. You won't come up with definitive answers like the scientists, but you may get a richer taste for life, an appreciation of it in a deeper way and a passion for all of life like the writer, artist,musician and (dare I say it!) the environmentalist!

Loosen up! Let yourselves go!

Death needs you!

I am Death and I figure in your life and the life of all that lives.

I have a bad reputation really, like I've got it in for everyone, but my intention is never to be mean and nasty. I have to work with what's there so sometimes I come in the form of disease, or in certain behaviours of human beings and animals that cause accidents or predation. I'm not that keen on these things but what can I do? They're not my choice! I prefer to visit you when you are old and ready to make the journey, so I can take you gently and give relief. But this side of things is not in my hands!

My role – if you would allow me to explain – is to accompany you on a journey into something which is quite mysterious to you and sometimes fraught with fear. That's because it's so unknown to you... in fact you have no idea!!! But I want to reassure you... you have no need to fear what awaits you. I can't give you details – that would be divulging professional secrets! But what I can say is that no one, as far as I know, has ever come back. Make of that what you will, but in my book it says 100% satisfaction! Pretty good odds, really!

The hardest part of my job is dealing with those who are left behind. The sadness they carry makes me weak at the knees. But what can **I** do??? That side of things I have to leave to others and I really need their help. So I guess that's why I'm talking with you, the reader. You are my unsuspecting assistants, caring for those on this side while I accompany those on the other side. We need to work together. I'm a bit relentless in my task, so I need you to be equally committed to yours. I don't have much choice in my work, but you can choose how you respond. In that respect you are more powerful than me.

Think about this now for I can tell you for sure that someone close to you will need your kindness and comfort before too long. Be prepared! Don't be caught off guard!

And don't think I'm just talking about human beings!

THE WIDOW'S MITE

A model of generosity or a story of exploitation?

SCRIPTURE

Mark 12:41-44

> He sat down opposite the treasury, and watched the crowd putting money into the treasury. Many rich people put in large sums. A poor widow came and put in two small copper coins, which are worth a penny. Then he called his disciples and said to them, 'Truly I tell you, this poor widow has put in more than all those who are contributing to the treasury. For all of them have contributed out of their abundance; but she out of her poverty has put in everything she had, all she had to live on'.

BACKGROUND

At the time of the writing of the New Testament, widows were not necessarily poor as there were some very influential widows in the early Christian communities. However, those without male protectors were vulnerable to exploitation and so were of special moral concern within the Law and the community. They often found themselves in a defenceless legal and financial situation.

Just prior to this story, Jesus is condemning the scribes for taking the homes of widows. This refers to a custom of naming a male relative to oversee the widow's affairs. However, this often ended in that person using her estate for his own benefit.

The widow in this story is invisible within her society; she gives what she has without making a song and dance about it. She does not seem to be concerned about how she will survive into the future. One interpretation is that it is faith that motivates her. The listener is then exhorted to be giving of one's very self, not just from what is left over.

Another interpretation of this story runs as follows: in the preceding passage, Jesus condemns the scribes who 'devour the houses of widows'. The widow's offering could be seen as part of a temple practice that exploits such women, encouraging them to give beyond what is sustainable, even to their last penny. The story then becomes a denunciation of the system that she is caught in and perhaps must support because of social and religious pressure.

Barbara Reid notes that this story could have been used as a warning not to act like the scribes. She also sees that it could be heard from different viewpoints.

> *"For those who would align themselves with the voracious scribes, it offers a challenge to reject all ways of feeding off the poorest, particularly under the guise of religion. For those who were oppressed and poor, it issues an invitation to reject giving support to those very systems that treat them unjustly."* [1]

REFLECTION

The musings of a banker

I had to appear at the Royal Commission into Misconduct in the Banking, Superannuation and Financial Services Industry today! What a waste of time! What do they think will come out of all this? The public are showing signs of shock and horror that our practices leave widows and single women homeless, that farmers are in debt that can never be repaid, that young people will never be able to own their own home for the foreseeable future, that we rip people off even after they're dead!

Let's get real. This is the world of business! We have hungry shareholders to face. They're forever wanting higher returns on their investments, regardless of what's happening in the real world. These investors act so innocently, as if they are somehow separate from this system we have and how it manages to keep producing ever greater profits for them. We're all embroiled in it. It's called capitalism! Actually, it's capitalism run riot... we bankers love it!

I've advised my colleagues to lie low for a while. They have us over a barrel at the Commission with all their forensic evidence, so I had to admit to a lot. It did feel a bit embarrassing when the Senior Counsel kept putting charges before me and asking if they were true. Embarrassment is not something I'm used to feeling, and I don't like it! They say criminal charges may be made, but my sense is that one or two heads will fall to placate the baying public, but once it is over and the news focuses on other things, I'm sure we'll get back to normal again. It's the system that lets us do these things. We are put under the microscope but the system is sacrosanct, not to be seriously questioned.

A poor widow muses

I came out of the Commission hearings today, more depressed than ever! I have lost my home because I followed bad investment advice from my bank that I have trusted since I first began working over forty years ago. I listened to the CEOs of several banks owning up to unbelievable behaviour with other people's money. Admission after admission, with straight faces and flat voices. There was no sense of shame at what they were doing or its implication for people like me who have lost everything. This would have all stayed hidden from the public eye had it not been for this Royal Commission. These people have no fear of God nor man! Then I heard a CEO apologising to the public on the news, mouthing changes that will be put in place to rectify 'mistakes' in the system, but no mention of the intentional behaviours and attitudes of entitlement throughout his business.

After being a woman of independent means, I now am forced to live with my son and his wife, not a particularly happy option. To feel like I am not a burden I have accepted minding their two small children so they can both work. I have cared for my children all my life and at this point I had hoped to have more freedom to explore things I haven't had the chance to do while my children were growing up. But that hope has all gone. The future doesn't look good for me. I'm still paying off debt and have nothing to show for it. I live at the pleasure and mercy of my son and his wife. There is no hope for me. At my age and now living on the pension, my options are nil. I guess I should be happy that at least I have a roof over my head, even if it belongs to someone else, and I have the means to put food on the table. There are widows like me in other parts of the world who have it harder. I feel ashamed to complain.

Two small coins...

That's us – the sum of what our owner has and she's about to give us away! What can we say to her?

She's going to put us into the Temple treasury to maintain this religious institution – even though she can hardly afford to live! Like so many women over the centuries, she has given more than her share to 'keep things going' but remains unnoticed, unsupported and discriminated against by the very same institution. But she doesn't see this, she just keeps giving!

Wake up, woman! Don't you see that we, small coins, have power! Withhold us, and encourage other women to do the same. Then the story will change. Without the financial contribution of women the institution will take notice – money is a powerful key to doors of power, including religious institutions.

So... hold us tightly in your hand for now. Don't let us go! We may help you be a catalyst for change!

The Woman Bent Over

Freeing a woman from more than her ailment.

SCRIPTURE

Luke 13:10-17

> Now he was teaching in one of the synagogues on the sabbath. And just then there appeared a woman with a spirit that had crippled her for eighteen years. She was bent over and quite unable to stand up straight. When Jesus saw her, he called her over and said, 'Woman, you are set free from your ailment.' When he laid his hands on her, immediately she stood up straight and began praising God. But the leader of the synagogue, indignant because Jesus had cured on the sabbath, kept saying to the crowd, 'There are six days on which work ought to be done; come on those days and be cured, and not on the sabbath day.' But the Lord answered him and said, 'You hypocrites! Does not each of you on the sabbath untie his ox or his donkey from the manger and lead it away to give it water? And ought not this woman, a daughter of Abraham whom Satan bound for eighteen long years, be set free from this bondage on the sabbath day?' When he said this, all his opponents were put to shame; and the entire crowd was rejoicing at all the wonderful things that he was doing.

BACKGROUND

Here is a story that symbolically offers an example of women bent over under the burden of patriarchy in all its forms and the bondage it holds them in throughout their lives. This story is unique to Luke, and while it is seen as a healing story it is interesting to note what Jesus says to this woman... He doesn't say 'You are healed.' but rather 'You are set free...' This stimulates thought with regard to the lack of freedom in the life of this woman. As readers in the 21st century, we may also wonder what freedom does Jesus offer us and call us to in the world of our own time.

Notice in this tale that the woman praises God not Jesus for her healing. The way it is told the healing of the woman appears to be attributed to Jesus rather than to God. But the woman doesn't get caught in this, she directs her praise and gratitude to God. As Schussler Fiorenza suggests, the ministry of Jesus was to make the liberating power of God experientially available to others,[1] which is what happens in this story. Her healing moves her from the margins to the centre, from invisibility and voicelessness to praise of God. It is God who has healed her and set her free and she does not cease to acknowledge it.

In this story, however, our attention is moved from this woman and what's happening to her to an argument between Jesus and the officials. Due to this shift of focus, the woman is no longer an active participant in the story but rather becomes an object of men's religious conflict. She has disappeared. And has remained so. Just as the focus moved from the woman to the argument, so too the experience of God in the coming to wholeness of this woman disappears and what comes into focus is who best keeps the laws of the tradition. Our attention as readers shifts from the liberation of this woman bent double to the observance of the law.

Here we have a healing story that transmutes into a controversy. It is likely that this reflects the tensions within the early Christian communities towards the end of the first century about who has authority to interpret the Word of God.

Also, a point for the reader to note is that Jesus doesn't answer the synagogue official's objection about coming on one of the other six days... So why on the sabbath? What's the Sabbath about? Traditionally, it's a time to stop in order to eat and drink, to celebrate and bless God who has created all things. Through this healing, Jesus has made it possible for this woman and the people to fulfil the purpose of the Sabbath-rest from work in order to praise God the creator and liberator of this woman.[2]

REFLECTION

Bent in half
seeing little, but hearing all
eighteen years have I suffered
old now and poor and a woman
nothing to excite the eyes of others
they turn away
I am an unperson, invisible in the crowd.
One moment of light falling on my path
bent no more,
seeing all, hearing all
a moment of grace, of encounter
and everything is changed
or so it seems....
My back is no longer bent
I stand straight up now as when I was young.
But I am still old and poor and a woman

unnamed
The joy of my healing does not sound
down the years
men's voices debating law take over
filling the air space, holding the focus.
I fall
into forgetfulness
no longer remembered -
not even for the sign
of God's desire realised in my wholeness –
lost, forgotten
Will you remember me? Please remember me
Rejoice with me? Please...
Give thanks with me? Please...

Walking along the busy main street in Amman, Jordan

I am enthralled with all around me. People are passing on their way home as I am, some carrying parcels or small children, others conversing with friends. The endless noise of the buses and traffic is such a normal background sound that it is no longer noticed. The footpath is crowded and I step off briefly to accommodate the approaching crowd when I notice a woman pass me by. She is covered in local flowing garments, almost invisible beneath them. Almost...

For a split second, her veil parts and I gain a momentary sight of her face. I remember it still after all these years! A face so disfigured she seemed hardly human! I turned to look after her as she disappeared within the crowd, but she was gone. And I was left speechless. What would life possibly be like for this woman, in a world where a woman's beauty is a bartering chip and a measure of her worth? What had happened to her? Was she born like this? Had she suffered burns? Beatings? Whatever its origin, her physical condition would certainly have caused her immeasurable suffering. A heavy burden... metaphorically enough to make one bend double under its weight.

My thoughts jumped and in my mind tumbled countless images of women's suffering throughout the world... women with untended fistulas after childbirth, women bought and sold in the markets of prostitution and pornography, women in service in countries far from their families in order to support them financially, women carrying experiences of rape as a tool of war and the signature of male power in all human societies, the subtle demeaning of women in sexist language and the male superiority that underlies it... even and especially within our churches... the images went on...

My thoughts returned to this veiled woman and I was left wondering how would I have carried such a burden in her place or in the face of any of these situations? Would I have been bent under its weight? And would there have been someone in my life to help me straighten up and find life anew?

Or perhaps my real question is... when do I choose to ease the burdens of another, to support their freedom so together we can walk straight?

The Great Barrier Reef cries under the weight...

We have lived here in these waters for millennia, experiencing the cycle of life, death and rebirth in an evolution that has felt it will have no end. Our colours have developed to make us spectacular and we are seen as one of the wonders of the world! Actually, we don't live with this awareness. We just live each day taken up in the natural flow of life.

But now the burden of human activity has interrupted all that. The acidification of the oceans, the raised water temperatures, the increased pollution... the list goes on... all adding to the weight that is crushing us. Some of us have been bleached so badly, there will be no return. We are bent double under this burden.

What happens to a living creature when it becomes overburdened with the impact of human beings? We cry out but not with the voice that humans have. All we have is our dead bodies, colourless now and no longer attractive to them. You can't make money out of dead coral and money is what counts! Isn't it?

Who among this horde of human beings will be the one to extend their hand and restore us to health as Jesus did in this story of the bent-over woman? Who will see us with his eyes and make such a response? A cure for an illness as grave as ours will require not just one person or even a few, it requires enough to form a mass that has the power to move others, especially those with political power.

We, the coral of the Great Barrier Reef, are waiting... and our time is running out.

Will you let us die with hardly a whimper?

The Sky...

Oh, how can I bear all that I am hearing today! The earth is trembling with the voices of despair, of death, of bewilderment. I survey this planet to see what's causing this ruckus.

I pass over Townsville and see a town submerged! For kilometres there is only water, no land in sight… cattle stranded in water and mud, farmers killing stock they had taken such great care of, weeping inconsolably as they witness the destruction before them. All of a sudden, my attention is drawn in another direction. My focus now is on parts of Tasmania and NSW as fire-fighters struggle against uncontainable fires, devouring forests, homes and possessions. The native animals are fleeing but they can't outrun this fire as it jumps across the landscape, spitting embers far ahead of it… My sight shifts again as it is drawn by a vast movement across the land… it is a dust storm crossing over those parts where water has not fallen for years. Its billows swirl like huge clouds, devouring all beneath it.

I have watched this planet develop from its earliest days, seen land form and fade away, species come and go. There is a human species at present… somewhat arrogant, still developing, but it worries me. Never have I seen such a wilfully destructive creature on the earth! In its naivety, it thinks nothing can harm it. It will solve all problems that present themselves! When will they come to their senses? What will it take for them to see how truly vulnerable they are?

People of the Amazon

"The indigenous peoples of the Amazon want to tell all of humanity that we are worried because due to the consequences of climate change the land is spoiling, the animals are shrinking, the trees are disappearing, the fish are dying, [and] the fresh water is running out."

Tribal leader Hector Sueyo of the *Harakbuti people* to Pope Francis

"We ask that you defend us!"

Tribal leader Yésica Patiachi of the *Harakbuti people* to Pope Francis

Woman with the Lost Coin

A woman personifies God's exuberant joy.

SCRIPTURE

Luke 15:1-3, 8-10

> Now all the tax collectors and sinners were coming near to listen to him. And the Pharisees and the scribes were grumbling saying, 'This fellow welcomes sinners and eats with them.' So he told them this parable....
>
> ... what woman having ten silver coins, if she loses one of them, does not light a lamp, sweep the house, and search carefully until she finds it? When she has found it, she calls together her friends and neighbours, saying 'Rejoice with me, for I have found the coin I had lost.' Just so, I tell you there is joy in the presence of the angels of God over one sinner who repents.

BACKGROUND

This small story forms part of a trio of things lost and found. It is a simple story only two verses long but within it we learn of the preciousness of the lost coin for the woman, her relentlessness in searching for it and her overflowing joy in finding it that must be shared with her neighbours. It is sandwiched between the story of the good shepherd and the lost sons. The first and third parts of the trio are well known but the woman's story seems to get sidelined. How often do we see works of art inspired by the first and third stories of this trio, how often do we see churches and organisations named after the good shepherd or hear references to this story and the same with the 'prodigal son'. Are there any churches named after the woman and her lost coin?[1] Even in western society where the holy dollar has almost idol status, this story remains hidden in a haze of forgetfulness.

One cannot but wonder why this is so. Is it because a coin is used as the lost 'thing' or is it that in the other two stories the main figure is male and usually understood to be a figure of God? So a problem arises when the main figure is a woman. This is unsettling! As we know, even today, our Tradition has a major problem imaging God in female form, so even when Jesus uses such an image we still have trouble giving it credence. Holding this story for us to read and think about is one way of reclaiming the truth that God is beyond gender and if represented in gendered form can be represented with equal validity in female as well as male form. Even St Augustine when giving a sermon on this parable began with "Holy Divinity has lost her money, and it is us!"[2]

Parables always have some twist in them, something that gives the reader/listener a shock so we stand back and look again at what we thought the story was about, having discovered something beyond what was expected. So in this story when the woman finds her coin she invites her neighbours and friends to come and celebrate with her. Her hospitality has a sense of generosity that probably exceeds the value of the drachma as she tries to express her joy at finding what was lost.

The lavishness of the woman's joy is what shocks. It is similar to that of the good shepherd and the loving father of the surrounding stories – all of them voicing the excitement, joy and delight of God when what was lost has been found and a relationship once broken is now restored.

The twist here is that God treasures us to the point of extravagance, beyond what would be 'normal' or 'reasonable' – intimating that this God that Jesus both experienced and shared, goes beyond anything we can conceive or imagine. As humans we tend to image God as a reflection of things/people we know, but this parable together with its companions says No! God and God's love for us are beyond anything we know – always richer, deeper, more tender, more faithful… It pulls us up and reminds us that our images are and always will be inadequate.

When reading this story, where does your attention go? The money and the search to find it? Or the woman who has responsibility for the family finances and is anxious over the loss of an amount of money? It can also be read metaphorically using this woman as a female image of God and how God acts in the world with a compassion that is relentless, boundary breaking, ready to celebrate us at every turn. This is a healthy reminder, especially in a Church where traditional images tend to be canonised and set in cement such as the image of God as father. This is human beings at work trying to capture something of God that fits neatly into our patriarchal world and set it as the limits of what is an acceptable image of God. However, our tradition is deeper and richer and if we listen carefully it will not let us settle for a fixed narrow image of God – let alone a singular masculine one. The presence of this woman in the story creates a fissure in the tightly held male image of God. She invites us to be open to surprise in our relationship with God…

Other metaphorical insights could also be explored… like, this woman could be us and we have lost something precious… When wondering what is lost, might we think broadly of what we as human beings have lost, such as our relationship to the natural world? A sense of the meaning of our place in the universe? What rejoicing might there be if we found a renewed, respectful relation to the other-than-human world around us. Would not the whole of the created universe ring with shouts of joy? The restoration of that relationship remains one of our most pressing and vital challenges of our day. The change in climate across the world and its fallout are a warning to us of the consequences of our continued alienation.

REFLECTION

Reflections on what has been lost... a human being muses in the presence of an attentive garden frog

Being a human being is quite extraordinary, even if I do say so myself! It's taken millions of years to make something like me. Frog, can I tell you our story?

Frog: I guess I'm going to hear it anyway!

Well, a long time ago (billions of years in fact), there was this big explosion and out of it came all the stuff that makes up the universe... elements, black holes, energies... lots of stuff! It was really hot but when it started to cool down then things like planets formed, and one of them was the place we call Earth, yes where we're sitting now. It did take a long time but eventually there was water and air and sunlight and all this helped life to begin to take shape in many different ways - amoeba, fish, reptiles, dinosaurs and eventually so many types of animals and trees and plants that you just couldn't count them. Yes, even **your** ancestors, my friend Frog!

Frog: Oh, this is interesting. Keep going!!

Well, these forms of life kept developing and changing so they could survive where they were living. And as they changed, some disappeared and some continued. Now among those that continued there was one sort of creature that branched off and kept changing until it eventually looked something like me! Its change, however, wasn't just in its looks; something was developing inside this creature that was a bit different from others. With respect, Frog, it wasn't that we were becoming better than you; we just had different capacities that kept growing. Like we started to think differently, with imagination and an awareness of an inner world. For a long time we were aware of belonging to the world in which we lived, we were a part of it and valued it because we realised we couldn't survive without a close relationship with it.

Frog: Yeah, that's normal enough!

But something happened that changed all that. I'm not sure when it began, but we humans... we started to look down on creatures like you. We were too smart and lost our way. So we didn't check our numbers, wanted more of everything and gradually forgot that we were part of Earth and became consumers of it. We lost our sense of kinship with the created world and saw creatures as meat to be eaten, trees as firewood or house materials, the oceans as dump yards for waste and land as a commodity to buy and sell. Yet in the middle of all this we kept looking for beauty. We had a sense that we were missing something really important... So people like me risk being seen as weird because I take the time to sit and chat with you. Can you believe that!? We've lost something very precious and don't even realise it!

Frog: What you've lost is only the beginning of the story... remember the woman and her lost coin? She didn't sit down and say 'Oh too bad, it will just have to stay lost!' No, she went searching, doing something about getting it back... and, of course, when she did get it back, there was the party!

Do you reckon we humans can get back this sense of kinship that we're missing?

Frog: You're a problematic species that's for sure, but you won't know unless you try!

God reflects on what has been lost...

Yes, this parable has got me thinking! Personifying me as a woman! I like that! Can't tell you how tired I am of this macho image of me... always a bloke, always strong, like a magic man who can do anything I'm asked! And making me the unmoving judge... that really leaves me with a deep sense of unease! There's an assumption that human beings know me and have me worked out. It's funny really... and when I hear them say 'God is an almighty father!', it really cracks me up!

Here is a story that shows me as a woman who has lost something she treasures and won't give up till she finds it. Even when it's out of sight she doesn't forget it. She really cares. That's something like me... not the whole picture... but a good addition! So what has been lost that I care about so much? Well I guess it's that human beings have lost a sense of me as the One who mothered them into being, the One who cherishes them beyond their wildest beliefs, who never gives up on them. When they come to know this in their bones, their relationship with me really changes. These are fresh, female images but Christian tradition has lost that sense and entrenches a tired, single male image of me. That's what has been lost, but I'm working hard to change this because it really matters! Now I just have to get those 'holy fathers' of the church to see me a bit differently! What odds would you give me?

Earth

I am bereft. I have become conscious in you, human beings, but now you have left me, gone your own way and severed our relationship!

Canaanite Woman

An unnamed foreign woman invites our engagement in a story of conflict and conversion.

SCRIPTURE

Matthew 15:21-28

> Jesus left that place and went away to the district of Tyre and Sidon. Just then a Canaanite woman from that region came out and started shouting, 'Have mercy on me, Lord, Son of David; my daughter is tormented by a demon.' But he did not answer her at all. And his disciples came and urged him, saying, 'Send her away, for she keeps shouting after us.' He answered 'I was sent only to the lost sheep of the house of Israel.' But she came and knelt before him, saying, 'Lord help me.' He answered, 'It is not fair to take the children's food and throw it to the dogs.' She said, 'Yes, Lord, yet **(but)** even the dogs eat the crumbs that fall from the their master's table.' Then Jesus answered her, 'Woman, great is your faith! Let it be done for you as you wish.' And her daughter was healed instantly.

BACKGROUND

This is a story – probably the only story in the Gospels where Jesus doesn't win an argument!

Elaine Wainwright[1] notes that there is ambiguity about the actual territory where the story takes place, leaving it unclear who is the resident and who is the foreigner, thus labelling them 'boundary-breakers'. Looking at it this way opens us up to various possibilities of what boundaries are being pushed in this story and who is pushing them? Boundaries of ethnicity, of gender, of who is in and who is out?

The woman is a Canaanite – bringing back memories of Rahab, one of the foremothers of Jesus. Not only is she a woman but also a foreigner, making her doubly marginalised in the Jewish worldview of the time. She is set within a story that raises the issue of the mission to the Gentiles – should the message of Jesus be preached beyond the Jewish community or not? In her person and her argument with Jesus, she not only opens up a future for her daughter but also for all those gentiles (including us!) who would come to faith in Jesus beyond the Jewish community.

There is a second issue running under this story as an undercurrent and it is the controversy of Jesus' mission to women. Does her request have legitimacy and is it

Jesus' mission (and that of his followers) to respond to her? The story is placed in the lifetime of Jesus and it is within his own struggle with his tradition and culture that he finds a resolution to these controversies.

As well, situating it in its historical time of writing and viewed through a feminist lens, the story represents the voice of women, speaking theologically, that has been repressed in the community. Jesus is presented as prejudiced and exclusive in his sense of identity. He doesn't particularly want to engage with this person who is both foreigner and a woman. And he throws a jibe at her about throwing the children's food to dogs, that has insulting overtones. But she persists and enters into a theological argument with him about where are the boundaries of God's graciousness to be drawn. Do they include only the Jews or do they extend beyond what can be imagined... even to the foreigner, the woman, the enemy, the unperson, the other-than-human?

Elisabeth Schussler Fiorenza draws our attention to the small word the woman uses in her reply to Jesus - the word 'but'. This little word opens up, both for Jesus in the story and for us as readers, a whole new way of seeing. We too, are invited to become 'boundary-breakers', going beyond narrow interpretations of our tradition or the tight confines of culture.

The interaction between the characters tends to take centre stage rather than the healing miracle itself. However, attention is required when reading this story as there is a tendency to focus on Jesus as the 'master' and the focus of action. When this is done we lose sight of the extraordinary challenge, insight and transformative action which this Canaanite woman shows.

REFLECTION

The Canaanite Woman writes to her sister Talliya.

My dear sister Talliya,

You who have been closest to me over the years since my daughter's birth; you who have sat with me during those dark hours – those long dark hours – when Anath was unwell and we thought we would lose her. It is to you that I write... I am beside myself with joy and don't know where or how to begin to share with you the things that have taken place on these days.

It all began when I was in the marketplace. Word was going around that this Jewish man – a healer – was in town. Anyway, you would know how I've been at my wit's end with Anath – trying everything known to make her better. She is approaching the age of womanhood and my greatest fear is that due to her condition we will not be able to find her a husband and I fear for her future.

So I took myself in hand and thought, 'What have I to lose?' I went looking for him and found him talking with some of his friends. You know I've never been slow in coming forward so I approached him, went right up close and began shouting and calling him names – honourable ones – to solicit his attention without offense. His friends were embarrassed and wanted to get rid of me – but you know me! I'm like a dog with a stick, I won't let it go! But this healer – Jesus – snubbed me and kept his back to me. He made a remark to his friends – I think it was about me not being Jewish. Anyway, I just kept calling out and Jesus said it wasn't fair to take the children's food and throw it to the dogs!

Well, by this stage, I was seeing red and was about to give as good as I got... but something stopped me in my tracks.

This was my last chance and I knew it.

A thought quickly came to me and leapt out of my mouth. I swear, Talliya, something had taken over me! I answered him that even the dogs can eat the crumbs that fall from the master's table!

As my words hit him, I could see a change happening. He looked at me directly now and recognised in my desperation something that connected us beyond the barriers – the many barriers – that would normally separate us. He crossed a boundary in himself at that moment. By giving myself a voice, I challenged the limits he was putting on the generosity of his God. He caught my drift. And with a graciousness that moved us both, he healed Anath.

She wasn't with me at the time but when I arrived home, I could see the difference in her immediately. It has been several weeks now, and she has had no further incidents of ill health. We are planning a celebration for her and we want you – her favourite (and only) aunt – to come and rejoice with us. Rejoice that in the body of this young woman we see traces of the mercy of this God of the Jews.

I hear that Jesus has stayed several days in our region and has been doing good wherever he goes. I wonder if, like us, he is rejoicing too!

Another angle from the woman from Canaan...

Well, I achieved well today. Hard work really... what's a woman to do in my circumstances? With an ill daughter and no money, I had to do what any mother would do... suck up!

Here was I at my wit's end when I noticed a commotion going on in the street. A healer had arrived in town but he was trying to stay out of public view. Fat chance in our town! You can't go out your front door without everyone knowing!

I walked down the street to see what was going on and I saw him standing there with locals around him. I was feeling desperate and wanted to get his attention before others took over, so I yelled, 'Have mercy on me, Lord, Son of David; my daughter is tormented by a demon.'

Yes, I had to call him 'Lord'... a lot of men like to be puffed up by others so I took a gamble. Good one really as it paid off! I got his attention alright but not easily. His evasive look and smart comment to me about not throwing the children's food to dogs was quite insulting. But I am a woman and I've had to put up with a lot of stuff like this from some men who see themselves as superior to women and can't resist a demeaning remark! But I wasn't going to be put off by this! Over the years, I've learnt a lot about humouring men. And now that I was in front of this great religious man, I would have to call on all my well-honed skills.

I met his comment with another of equal astuteness, using the word 'Master'. You see, I was playing the game... You know the one, women play it as second nature... where you humour the bloke, beg for crumbs, act gratefully, appear submissive. Yes, that's it... the 'suck-up' game!

It's a tricky game really for women to play. A bit of a two-edged sword. When we do it a lot, we can come to believe that we really are second class and barely deserve the crumbs. It takes a lot of thought and nous to play it and not get entangled. I did alright today. I could have done more... perhaps challenged Jesus' racial prejudice and sexism in a forthright way. But I walked the knife-edge... and got what I needed.

Actually, I'm not sure he needed me to play the game. He was different from other men I'd known, and while he needed stretching, he was able to meet the challenge! We both gained more from this exchange than we expected!

A Twenty-first century Catholic reflects on this story...

I'm listening to this Canaanite woman and how she gets what she needs in a patriarchal world where she is seen and treated as second class. My thoughts then wander to today and what it's like being a woman in the Catholic Church… there's a lot of similarities! The assumption of male entitlement and privilege runs so deep.

I'm thinking of the Leadership Conference of Women Religious in the US and their engagements with the bishops who put them under investigation. The assumption the bishops held of their unquestioned and unaccountable authority, together with their use of power to attempt to stifle what did not suit their religious and political positions was on show for all to see. What was equally astounding was the thoughtful and prayerful approach the women took in their responses to the bishops over a period of years. No 'sucking up' game here! But rather an on-going invitation to a mutual listening and exchange. These women held their position as full members in the Catholic Church, with voice and agency. While being respectful of authority, they did not take a subservient position but one of equality and adult, mutual respect.

These women said the proverbial 'but' and showed us how women have been and continue to be alive and full members of the Church today without acquiescing to male abusive power.

BUT… but… but

On women sharing the sacrament of ordination with men "The church has spoken and says no… that door is closed." Pope Francis

But… but… if priesthood is about service, are women not eminently qualified for it? Human cultures have relegated women to the servant role for millennia!

Canon 1024: A baptised male alone receives sacred ordination validly.

But…but… who made this rule? And why is it not open to change as Tradition and practice have been over time? Is it not a rule made by men to self perpetuate their own positions of power and deny a place for women?

Canon 1008: By divine institution, the sacrament of orders establishes some among the Christian faithful as sacred ministers… They are consecrated and designated each according to his grade, to nourish the people of God, fulfilling in the person of Christ the Head the functions of teaching, sanctifying and governing.

But…but… what in the roles of teaching, sanctifying and governing are beyond the capacities of women?

Women's Persistence for Justice

The persistence of a woman seeking justice becomes an image of how God acts.

SCRIPTURE

Luke 18:1-8

> Then Jesus told them a parable about their need to pray always and not to lose heart. He said, 'In a certain city there was a judge who neither feared God nor had respect for people. In that city there was a widow **who kept coming to him** and saying, 'Grant me justice against my opponent.' For a while he refused; but later he said to himself, 'Though I have no fear of God and no respect for anyone, yet because this woman keeps bothering me, I will grant her justice, so that she may not wear me out by continually coming.'
>
> And the Lord said, 'Listen to what the unjust judge says. And will not God grant justice to his chosen ones who cry to him day and night? Will he delay long in helping them? I tell you, he will quickly grant justice to them. And yet, when the Son of Man comes, will he find faith on earth?'

BACKGROUND

Judges were elders in the community with the expectation that they would exercise their role with integrity and uprightness. However, the judge in this story is said to have fear of neither God nor people, meaning that his behaviour was not regulated by the opinion of others nor religious expectations. He was a law unto himself, without care for his reputation or honour. He seems used to a judicial practice that possibly uses a system of taking bribes in favour of the interests of the rich and sells women like this widow short.

In the patriarchal culture of first century Judaism, being a widow meant more than the loss of one's husband. It often meant that the woman was now either dependent on other male members of her husband's family and therefore at their mercy, or she was now outside the normal social structure where women lived under the authority of some male. This meant that she was responsible for herself without the social and familial protections accorded to other women. This left her vulnerable to exploitation and injustice.

Because of their vulnerable position, widows would usually be expected to keep a low profile and not to be a bother to anyone.

Most biblical scholars see this story as including both Jesus' original parable, as well as a layer of interpretation added by the Gospel writer. They suggest that verses 2-5 are most likely closest to Jesus' original parable.[1]

Parables are a particular form of storytelling. There is usually a twist that holds some level of shock for the listener. In this parable, the shock comes in several ways. The characters are not what the listener would be expecting from the stereotype of these characters. The judge who holds a high and respected rank seems to have no moral compass and the widow, who is usually seen as vulnerable and unprotected, is a feisty woman. She is no wall flower but rather the text says, 'she kept coming', determined to get justice. Being poor, she is not in a position to offer the judge a bribe to make him do his job. All she has is her voice and a dogged determination not to be fobbed off. The tactic she uses is not to criticise the judge but rather to keep demanding that he do his duty.

The judge finally gives her what she is seeking on the grounds that he doesn't want her to 'wear him down'. The Greek verb used here (*hypopiazo*) is a boxing term that could be translated as 'to give someone a black eye'! Again, there is shock at such a description of what the judge is genuinely afraid of in his encounter with this woman. There is also a humourous element in the image of this powerful judge cowering before a defenceless widow. She is pestering him publicly and ceaselessly. He wants to get rid of her before things escalate, not because he has changed from his corrupt ways. The persistence of this widow reminds us of Tamar and Ruth. These women from Jesus' foremothers also showed courage and creativity in achieving justice within their own situations.

The Gospel writer tells this story from a traditional patriarchal position in that it is automatically assumed that the male figure is taken as the God image and the supplicant woman as representative of us when we come to petition God in prayer.

However, Barbara Reid sees a further twist or shock here when she interprets the woman as an image of God - persistently seeking justice for the poor![2] Talking about God in female images would have been unsettling to the readers of this Gospel, as it continues to be in the Church today! So, taking on the female identity, does God then become a 'nag' as ordinary women who are persistent in their demands are often labelled?

The Gospel writer takes this parable and uses it to suggest to his listeners how one should be persistent in prayer. By putting this parable in the context of prayer rather than in the relentless demands for justice, Reid suggests that Luke is actually trying to domesticate this unconventional and pesty woman. Not unlike his story of Martha and Mary, he prefers women to stay in the quieter and less disturbing position of listeners and pray-ers rather than disturbing the peace and the male order by breaking social boundaries and persistently raising their voices in the pursuit of justice. She also suggests that the ridiculousness of this image of the judge caving in to the 'power' of the widow may have been a tongue in cheek comment from the historical Jesus about the futility of using violence in the pursuit of justice.

What may we learn from this pesky woman? Barbara Reid offers one possibility...

"This parable, with its unusual characters and startling ending, jolts the hearer into a new way of seeing. It asks one to leave behind stereotypes and wrestle with the unfamiliar notions about what God is like and what justice in the realm of God looks like and how it is achieved. It invites one to emulate such a pursuit of justice in efforts to embody the reign of God here and now while awaiting future fulfilment."[3]

REFLECTION

Prayer of the widow

God of our ancestors, you who have given us laws to protect the vulnerable and those without help. Hear my prayer as I face this judge who is in league with my adversary. How can I possibly find justice when everything seems stacked against me? I am a woman and without male protection. Without this property settlement, I have nothing to support myself and my children. I'm desperate and have nowhere else to take my distress. We sing of your faithfulness in the morning and at night; let me taste it in my life! Do not leave me for dead!

God's prayer to the widow

Beloved! You know from the long story of my engagement with you and your people that I hear the cry of the poor and will come swiftly to be at your side in this dispute. Your case is lost only if you believe it futile and give up. Your feisty character is my gift to you. Use it well and be persistent. When you are pesky in seeking justice, you are like me! Do not be afraid!

Judgment Day...

She woke up early this day. The sun was shining and she could feel the determination rise within her. 'Today's the day!' she said to herself. She dressed quickly, took her meagre breakfast and left her house. The road was beginning to be crowded with people as the morning bustle began. She headed straight to the city gate, calling on all her foremothers, all those who had been widowed and were in dire straits as she was, to cheer her on in what she was about to do, to give her the courage she needed.

Every two weeks, the Judge arrived to hear cases of dispute or to deal with any problems in the community. He was a fearsome man, having no respect for tradition, for people or for God. He was well known for his prejudice and his quickness to take a bribe to settle a case in favour of the one paying.

The Judge knew this woman and recognised her as she came closer. There was something different about her today. Her stride was strong and determined and he noticed her fists were clenched. A feeling of uneasiness came over him. Was she going to cause a scene? For months now she had been coming to seek justice in her property dispute, hoping to retain possession of her house. She was a widow without a male relative even to accompany her to this court hearing. With no one to protect her, she was an easy target for exploitation. And he, as judge, had been assisting those seeking to take advantage of her.

While he had no particular care for others, he did have a weak spot for how he appeared before them. If this woman caused a scene it could mean a significant loss of face. How would it look if a woman, and a widow at that, was to give him a black eye!

She approached the back of the crowd. Usually she would wait quietly until she was called, but not today. She snaked her way through the crowd, using her elbows when necessary. And before she knew it she stood there in front of him. Before he had the chance to begin the first case, she raised her voice for all to hear, demanding that he, the judge, act justly and according to the law, that he stop taking bribes and act honourably. He tried to brush her aside and begin the awaiting case, but she would not be silenced. Again and again she raised her voice and each time with greater strength. The judge noticed that her fists remained clenched and that she was moving ever closer. If she, a poor widow, was to become violent with him he would lose face badly and his reputation would be in tatters. He could not afford such an outcome.

She did not know where her strength had come from but her persistence won out and here was this fearsome man pronouncing a decision in her favour! He was talking quickly and brushing her aside to avoid attention. Could she believe her ears? Had these long months of dispute really come to an end? So quickly and favourably?

It felt like she was walking a metre off the ground as she returned home, a prayer of thanks on her lips and a heart pounding with joy and relief.

God speaks... in praise of nagging!

When injustice raises its head, when corruption robs the poor of their rights, when Earth is raped and abused... do not stay silent, cowering in fear. Take heart, be persistent in your resistance, be a nag! Raise your voice in every place, before your peers, before the powerful, nag, nag, nag. Leave weapons and violence aside. Your voice, raised on the streets, printed in newspapers, posted on social media, spoken at home and abroad, will be your fiercest weapon. Wherever there's a chance, badger, hassle, pester! Don't give up! When you act this way you are acting like me!

A Woman anoints Jesus

A woman's disturbing and prophetic action.

SCRIPTURE

Matthew 26:6-13

> Now while Jesus was at Bethany in the house of Simon the leper, a woman came to him with an alabaster jar of very costly ointment, and she poured it on his head as he sat at the table. But when the disciples saw it, they were angry and said, 'Why this waste? For this ointment could have been sold for a large sum, and the money given to the poor.' But Jesus, aware of this, said to them, 'Why do you trouble the woman? She has performed a good service for me. For you always have the poor with you, but you will not always have me. By pouring this ointment on my body she has prepared me for burial. Truly I tell you, wherever this good news is proclaimed in the whole world, what she has done will be told in remembrance of her.'

BACKGROUND

This anointing takes place at the beginning of the passion narrative. The unnamed woman anoints Jesus' head, a prophetic gesture used for the anointing of kings. Some interpretations also see this as an anointing prior to Jesus' death, that is, as an anointing for burial in an attempt to counter the disgrace of Jesus' criminal burial.

Elaine Wainwright[1] offers a hypothesis that this story carries an important historical memory held by the community in which Jesus was anointed in a cultic fashion by a woman prior to his death, together with the strong reaction of those present. She poses the question as to why her action was greeted with indignation. If she was simply performing an action of respect or honour towards Jesus, it would probably not have elicited such a response from the disciples. However, if by such an anointing she was enacting a prophetic function that belonged to men, it would most certainly have evoked a reaction. She also notes that it is the male disciples, representatives of 'authoritative tradition' who object to the woman's action.

In this story, Jesus responds to the disciples' negative reaction by defending the woman and praising her action. The historical memory held by the community goes even further in that it may point to the historical Jesus crossing social and religious boundaries in order to include women as full and active participants in this new community forming around him. Wainwright takes another step and suggests that Jesus also supported the courage and initiative of such women who dared to cross those boundaries themselves.

The story of the disciples' dismissive treatment of this woman reminds us of a similar scene earlier in Matthew's Gospel (15:21-28). We recall there that the disciples attempted to send the Canaanite woman on her way. In this anointing story, the male disciples once again shift attention away from what this woman is actually doing. It raises the question yet again, could the position and activity of women in the early Christian community have been a significant issue? One where women were claiming legitimacy based on the actions of Jesus himself, and one being actively opposed within the community?

This story would have had powerful political overtones to the ears of listeners at that time as it does today. It is not surprising, then, that it gets toned down by raising a different question regarding the costliness of the ointment and the issue of responsibility to the poor, a more traditional concern than the volatile issue of what women were doing.

Some scholars suggest the word 'waste' in this story is more accurately translated as 'destruction'. So the question on the lips of the disciples would be more like... Why this destruction? This may explain why there was such indignation at the woman's action, at her overwhelmingly presumptuous behaviour, that was destroying the social customs already embedded within their culture and world view.

REFLECTION

The woman finds her voice...

'Truly I tell you, wherever this good news is proclaimed in the whole world, what she has done will be told in remembrance of her.'

Well, this is what the Gospel says, but it's not true! When do you ever hear this story of me? And how do you remember me in it when my name is not even mentioned!

I actually have a name... it is Miriam. I am one of the women who have followed Jesus since early in his public life. We don't get much mention even though there were quite a number of us. This story says nothing about me as a person or how I came to be at Simon's house. So let me fill you in on the details!

I am saying this to you long after the events of this story took place. Jesus was executed and came to new life, the community of disciples has continued to grow and we are forming into a recognisable group. But as time is passing, there is tension in the group. Some are saying that what Jesus said and did in relation to women was too radical and that we need to tone it down 'a bit'! Women have been continuing their roles as leaders of house churches, preaching and accompanying men on journeys to spread the good news and this is raising the ire of some who are trying to quash the freedom of the women disciples and make them conform to the place our culture says belongs to them. But the women are resisting and when this Gospel was written the memory of the stand Jesus took has found a voice, probably because of pressure from the women. They remembered the day I came to Jesus at Simon's place and anointed him...

Things were heating up and those who were opposed to Jesus among the officials were looking for a way to 'deal' with him. We could all feel it. You didn't need to be a scholar to see where things were leading. So I wanted to do something for him to comfort him and relieve some of the tension in him. Jesus' response was to encourage such acts of kindness. It was as simple as that really. But, later, Matthew took up this memory and used it to make a point about supporting the freedom of women to be and act as disciples without the restrictions that some were wanting to place on them.

Yes, Jesus was pretty clear on all this but it's not going down well with some. Male privilege and entitlement run pretty deep! My sense is that this battle won't be solved for a long time!

Jesus addresses himself

Oh, how good it is to be out in the fields for a bit, away from all the chatter and disputes! I've been a bit preoccupied. Peter and the others are giving me grief. Even when I make it clear to them that what I'm on about is a community of equals, they simply don't get it. Even among the blokes, they are vying for who will be top dog, but when it comes to seeing the women as their equals... well forget it! Asking them to share both power and responsibility with the women is like...asking them the impossible! They will believe in a God they can't see, and they'll accept such things as the resurrection of the dead, but they are really struggling with the fact that God does not distinguish on the basis of gender, and so treats everyone equally!

What do I do with them?

Oil

The fruit of olives
crushed
I now am poured over the head
of this man
to soothe
strengthen
anoint
perhaps for burial
of course
what else could it be for?
this man is on a collision course
a one-way trip.
Let me then soak in
gently
refreshing
vivifying
as his time runs out...

A WOMAN
ANOINTS
JESUS

WOMEN WITNESSES OF THE CRUCIFIXION

Women witnessing, staying present, keeping vigil...

SCRIPTURE

Matthew 27:45-61

From noon on, darkness came over the whole land until three in the afternoon. And about three o'clock Jesus cried out with a loud voice, 'Eli, Eli, lema sabachthani?' that is, 'My God, my God, why have you forsaken me?' When some of the bystanders heard it, they said, 'This man is calling for Elijah.' At once one of them ran and got a sponge, filled it with sour wine, put it on a stick, and gave it to him to drink. But the

others said, 'Wait, let us see whether Elijah will come to save him.' Then Jesus cried again with a loud voice and breathed his last. At that moment the curtain of the temple was torn in two, from top to bottom. The earth shook, and the rocks were split. The tombs also were opened, and many bodies of the saints who had fallen asleep were raised. After his resurrection they came out of the tombs and entered the holy city and appeared to many. Now when the centurion and those with him, who were keeping watch over Jesus, saw the earthquake and what took place, they were terrified and said, 'Truly this man was God's son.'

Many women were also there, looking on from a distance; they had followed Jesus from Galilee and had provided for him. Among them were Mary Magdalene, and Mary the mother of James and Joseph, and the mother of the sons of Zebedee (James and John).

When it was evening, there came a rich man from Arimathea, named Joseph, who was also a disciple of Jesus. He went to Pilate and asked for the body of Jesus; then Pilate ordered it to be given to him. So Joseph took the body and wrapped it in a clean linen cloth and laid it in his own new tomb, which he had hewn in the rock. He then rolled a great stone to the door of the tomb and went away. **Mary Magdalene and the other Mary were there, sitting opposite the tomb.**

BACKGROUND

In this story, Joseph of Arimathea, and not one of the twelve apostles, comes to take Jesus' body and bury it. Crucifixion was a cruel and humiliating punishment in the Roman World. Bodies were left in the open after death or put into a mass grave. Joseph's request for permission to take Jesus' body suggests a concern to avoid further shame to Jesus' family and community of followers.

In the midst of the horror that is crucifixion, we see a group of women who followed Jesus from Galilee, present and watching on from a distance. One would have expected the twelve apostles to be there somewhere, but it is the women who take up their call to discipleship and remain to the end. Like the 'Women in Black' who hold vigils all over the world in the pursuit of justice and peace today, these women keep vigil at the cross and at the tomb when all seems lost.

Among these faces is the mother of the sons of Zebedee (James and John). Earlier in this Gospel (20:20-22), it is she who comes with her sons to seek a key position for them in the coming kingdom as they imagine it. Jesus asks her and her sons at that time if they are prepared to drink the cup of suffering, a call to discipleship which they accept. She, alone, remains here as a faithful disciple with the other women, supporting and consoling each other as they keep vigil. But her sons have fled. James will later be killed by Herod, so this woman's grief will continue... Will she in turn be consoled by these women who stand with her, looking on from a distance as Jesus is executed?

The other two women named are Mary Magdalene and Mary the mother of James and Joseph. John places both women at the cross and at the tomb. With two exceptions, these are the only women who are identified by name in John's entire Gospel. Generally, it is unusual for the writers of the gospels to single out women by naming them. When they are named as these women are, it indicates what an important place they hold in the life and death of Jesus and in the memory of the early Christian community. [1]

REFLECTION

Mary Magdalene and Mary the mother of James look back on their shared experience:

Fidelity is not an easy choice...

As we stood together watching the tortuous death of our friend and teacher, we were stretched to out limits... limits of strength, of endurance. We did not want to be there, we did not want this to be happening. We wanted to scream, to protest, but to do anything like this would endanger us all. We were living under occupation. Do you know what that's like? You are caught in a net, and can be strangled at any time, so to speak. Life is arbitrary and even when it feels ok, it can change in an instant and at the whim of the powerful.

So we stood at a distance, doing the very little that was in our power to do... to witness, to be present...to keep vigil...

Mary the mother of James and Joseph

As the aunt of Jesus, I followed him closely. To begin with I didn't always agree with him, but as time went on I got onto his wavelength and became very supportive. That's how come I travelled with him and a group of his followers to Jerusalem.

Mary Magdalene, Zebedee's wife and myself had become good friends. And so we stood together at a distance and witnessed something that no human being should witness. Crucifixion is one of the most inhumane ways of treating another human being regardless of what they had done. So how much more so when the one being crucified was an innocent man! We stood there huddled together, holding in our grief, our anger and disbelief. Some of us had seen him as a young boy running and playing with his mates, growing to adulthood and maturity following the death of Joseph. He had always had something different about him. His refusal to use violence of any form to impose himself on others, his optimism even in the face of occupation and his talk about God was different from anything we had heard from our leaders and teachers. We all wondered where he got it from and what would become of him. And today we saw...

Wisdom/Sophia speaks...

I, who was at play with God in the creation of the world am speechless before what I am witnessing in the execution of this man! These human beings who are the fruit of our work over billions of years should come to this! As I scan the scene, I am repulsed by the cruelty; I shudder at the callousness that is before me.

But there is something else present here in the midst of such horror... I notice some women at the side, keeping vigil, refusing to flee or to abandon this One whom they have followed. And even when the spectacle is over and everyone has gone, here are two of them waiting, keeping watch... In one sense it is such a simple thing to do but I am heartened by the love I see here ... strong, courageous, faithful love. Embodied love. Human beings have a saying that it is love that moves the sun and stars but I say... love like this moves both the universe and God's very self!

Earth

And I see this sort of love in the simple wonder and care with which some human beings respond to me... even in the face of insatiable growth capitalism, they continue to care, protest my demise, struggle on my behalf. What courage!

Mary Magdalene at the Tomb

Mary Magdalene invites the reader into a journey of faith with her.

SCRIPTURE

John 20:11-18

> But Mary stood weeping outside the tomb. As she wept, she bent over to look into the tomb, and she saw two angels in white, sitting where the body of Jesus had been lying, one at the head and the other at the feet. They said to her, 'Woman, why are you weeping?' She said to them, 'They have taken away my Lord, and I do not know where they have laid him.' When she had said this, she turned round and saw Jesus standing there, but she did not know that it was Jesus. Jesus said to her, 'Woman, why are you weeping? Whom are you looking for?' Supposing him to be the gardener, she said to him, 'Sir, if you have carried him away, tell me where you have laid him, and I will take him away.' Jesus said to her, 'Mary!' She turned and said to him in Hebrew, 'Rabbouni!' (which means Teacher). Jesus said to her, 'Do not hold onto me, because I have not yet ascended to the Father. But go to my brothers and say to them, 'I am ascending to my Father and your Father, to my God and your God.' Mary Magdalene went and announced to the disciples, 'I have seen the Lord', and she told them that he had said these things to her.

BACKGROUND

The Gospel of John, from where this story comes, was written with a clear purpose. The writer says it is written so that we, the readers, may come to faith and be transformed. Not faith in certain tenets of belief or in an institution, but in a living relationship with the Christ that leads to the quality of human life he lived and shared. All four gospels agree that women were the primary witnesses to Jesus' death, burial and the empty tomb and that the first resurrection appearance was to Mary Magdalene. This gives weight to the likelihood that this story is authentic historically. This part of the story carries an underlying question 'Where is the Lord?' Like many of us following the death of someone close to us, we ask a version of this question... Where is... now? It is Mary Magdalene who voices it both for herself and for us, as through this story we face, with her, the horror and shame of the crucifixion.

In Sandra Schneiders' beautiful insight into this story, she notes that the 'where' that is being searched for is not a particular location, but rather it is to do with the indwelling or communion between God, Jesus and his disciples. When Mary Magdalene poses the question 'Where is the Lord?', at one level the answer is that he is with God.

However, in this story another answer emerges... Jesus has returned to his own. John reveals how Mary's understanding develops in stages. What this means and how it comes about, John answers in three steps. The first step begins with Mary weeping. The second step happens at the 'turning' which is not a physical movement because in the story she is already facing Jesus. It is an inner turning from what had been familiar before the crucifixion and resurrection of Jesus to a new way of being and seeing that happens in the life of the person who comes to faith. The third step is in the activity of 'announcing' when Mary goes to the disciples and announces that she has seen the Lord.[1]

The writer of this Gospel has used powerful symbolism in this part of the story. It is set in a darkened garden before sunrise, capturing the inner experience of the disciples after their leader and teacher has been executed. The garden evokes the Garden of Eden and the story of creation, while the figure of Mary Magdalene weeping calls to mind the Beloved in the Song of Songs. These cues set the scene for the encounter with the risen Jesus 'the liberator of the new creation and the spouse of the people with the woman Mary Magdalene, symbol of the community of the gospel writer, and of us who engage with his writing today.[2]

Seeking Jesus and coming to faith is the heart of John's Gospel and Mary Magdalene embodies this search and journey into faith. However, her grief blinds her and she does not recognise him when he stands before her. The writer skilfully prepares us to make the journey with Mary from a preoccupation with Jesus' physical presence to an openness to a new mode of presence brought about in what we refer to as resurrection. The writer alerts us to this change by using the word 'turning'. This action as we have noted, does not refer to a change in her bodily orientation as the text already has her facing Jesus who she thinks is the gardener.

"Jesus said to her, 'Mary!' **Turning** she said to him, in Hebrew, 'Rabbouni.'

The change or turning happens when she hears her name and she calls him 'Teacher' which is an expression of the faith that the whole gospel seeks to evoke from its readers.

The journey does not end at this point; rather, it opens out into a whole new dimension when Mary is commissioned to go to the disciples and announce what she has come to know and believe. John's Gospel has an ongoing thread calling us to the truth that our relationship with God is one of intimacy, alive and vibrant. This is what Mary Magdalene is sent to announce to the disciples of her day and to the disciples of each age as we continue to read her story.

REFLECTION

Mary Magdalene remembers...

It is many years now since all these events happened. And even though I am old and frail, my memory has stayed sharp. When I look back to that time, I can still feel it in my body... the distress, the grief and the bewilderment. Then my encounter with him in the garden! At first it made me think that all we'd been through was just a bad dream. But no, it had all been real and so was he as he stood there before me! I wanted to go and hold him as before, but something stopped me. There was a difference now, and I didn't understand it. In fact, it has taken me a long time to understand the experience of those days...

Yes, I had been close to Jesus. We shared an experience of the divine and could talk about it without fear or taboos. Our experience of God impacted on our whole lives in ways we could share and question and explore. This created a very special bond... a bond I came to realise would be sustained beyond death, a bond that sustained me in the face of discrimination and attempts to silence me. Peter struggled with my presence in the group around Jesus and the things Jesus shared with me. It was as if I was in competition with him. Only if my voice was silenced would I no longer be perceived as a threat to him, so my voice needed to be silenced. Peter never seemed to understand that there was no need for competition. The expansiveness of Jesus' love... and God's...meant that there was more than enough room for all of us without having to pit one against the other!

As our movement grew, there were attempts to silence me. And later generations would continue their attempts at silencing my voice in the wider community by calling me a prostitute! A very effective way of discrediting a woman!

But I would not be silenced... not then...not now...

Zebedee's wife speaks...

I am the mother of the sons of Zebedee. The gospels don't give me a name. They refer to me only in terms of my relationship to the men in my life! I am a friend of Mary Magdalene and when she came to tell us what had happened to her in the garden, we shared her bewilderment and joy. She told us about the mission she had been given and wanted me to accompany her to see the other disciples. On our way, we mused together about all the events of recent days. We wondered where this would take us all.

As we approached the meeting place with the disciples, our excitement mounted.

Andrew was the first to greet us as we entered. Mary called the disciples together and began talking them through all she had experienced.

Her reception was underwhelming to say the least! In fact, the disciples weren't keen to accept her account at all! They protested and even got a bit personal in their criticism of her. Jesus had to visit them several times to reassure them that what Mary had said was true. It took a while, but eventually they began to get a sense of what resurrection was about.

Some elements of our group continued to give her a hard time. The journey to faith is a difficult one and each person has their own road to take. Some people can allow for the differences while others can't. And the closeness of Mary's relationship with Jesus just seemed to cause problems with some!

Angel

I am one of the unnamed angels sitting in the tomb when Mary of Magdala arrived. There was another angel there with me too (also unnamed). We were on duty, keeping watch. We weren't too sure what we were on watch for, so it was good when Mary arrived and there was a bit of action! It had been a long night and things had been pretty quiet. In spite of what artists have depicted throughout the ages, resurrection is a very quiet process... no fanfares, no trumpets...

We watched on as Mary encountered the risen Christ. It was a classic really... how she came to such a deep faith both in the person of Jesus and in the God of her people. I really liked this woman! She had a feistiness about her and a depth that was intriguing to me as an angel.

When Jesus said to her to go and tell the disciples that she had seen him, I thought to myself... this is going to be interesting!! These guys were having trouble all along in actually getting what Jesus was about. Peter started to get it at the last supper when Jesus washed his feet, but there was still a lot of resistance in him... understandably... Jesus was asking of them something way outside the norm.

In the meantime, once Mary cottoned onto this new reality, my friend and I were free to go! Not a bad night's work really. Meeting this woman and seeing her transformation made it all worth it!

Peter

Gee, women let their imaginations run away with them!!

Mary has just been here with an unbelievable story about seeing Jesus in the garden where he was buried a couple of days ago! The other Apostles and I all agree that she's well and truly lost it! She's been telling everyone and stirring up people's hope. I'm going to have to pull rank on her as this could get out of hand altogether. This woman, and others like her, are getting a bit uppish and need to know their place. It might take some time to tie them down, but it must be done!

Earth

This Jesus was laid to rest within me, as so many of you are... a quiet, cool place after the noise and trauma leading to his death.

Human beings who are Christians have a text called the Apostles Creed and it says that Jesus went down into hell to bring out all those that were chained and bound, to bring them freedom. So human beings think that this transformation they call resurrection just applies to them! But let me tell you it goes way...way beyond that!

Some accounts say that I shook... I guess that's one way of talking about it. Yes, I shook... out of delight, out of amazement, out of joy! I have been spinning here in the darkness of the universe for a long time, going through endless processes of change and development and wondering where on earth is this all leading! So when I shook that day I gained a small insight into the answer to my wondering. Nothing like a road map, more like an intuition of something that I was not able to see clearly or explain. But the shaking in me held a sense of excitement, of overwhelming delight, of a future full of plenty and abundance for all forms of life. You human beings are only one of these forms but you have become very powerful, and somewhat reckless in your use of it. For many of the creatures that would inhabit me, there will be no life and no resurrection because of you... Do you ever think of this? Does it concern you at all?

Jesus

"Don't hold onto me... don't cling to me..." is what I said to her and was I delighted when she got it!

This was the whole pattern of my life and my death and it is the pattern that allows created beings to enter into the flow of God's abundant love... this love that surrounds and upholds us even when we are not aware of it. I had experienced this love and learnt that clinging to things, people, reputation... anything in fact blocked the flow of this love and its power in our lives. Later generations misunderstood this as a penitential practice, but that was missing the point altogether. What I was saying in my words and in my living was that nothing had to be renounced, everything could be embraced, but the key was not to cling... to anything!

And Mary got it… but her insight was seen as so radical that she was given a hard time and virtually silenced. And this important moment of letting go was reduced and distorted into 'not having', 'doing without'.

But this little encounter in the garden that the writer of John's Gospel has retained is a gem that holds the invitation that I wanted to give to everyone on their life's journey… Don't cling…. and all will be yours!

Mary Magdalene and her companions hurry to share the news of Jesus' resurrection with Peter and the other disciples.

Epilogue

SOPHIA WISDOM

Sophia/Wisdom: female image of God from the Book of Proverbs. She delights in the creation of the world and is the companion of all life forms, including humans.

SCRIPTURE

Wisdom of Solomon 7:7-12, 22-23, 27 to 8:1

> Therefore I prayed, and understanding was given me; I called on God, and the spirit of wisdom came to me. I preferred her to sceptres and thrones, and I accounted wealth as nothing in comparison with her. Neither did I liken her to any precious gem, because all gold is but a little sand in her sight, and silver will be accounted as clay before her. I loved her more than health and beauty, and I chose to have her rather than light, because her radiance never ceases.
>
> All good things came to me along with her, and in her hands uncounted wealth. I rejoiced in them all, because wisdom leads them; but I did not know that she was their mother...
>
> There is in her a spirit that is intelligent, holy, unique, manifold, subtle, mobile, clear, unpolluted, distinct, invulnerable, loving the good, keen, irresistible, beneficent, humane, steadfast, sure, free from anxiety, all-powerful, overseeing all, and penetrating through all spirits that are intelligent, pure and all together subtle...
>
> Although she is but one, she can do all things, and while remaining in herself, she renews all things; in every generation she passes into holy souls and makes them friends of God, and prophets; for God loves nothing so much as the person who lives with wisdom.
>
> She reaches mightily from one end of the earth to the other, and she orders all things well.

REFLECTION

As we come to this part of our reflections, there is one more story that needs to be told and highlighted. It is THE story that underpins all other stories... it is the story of our origins, where we have come from, how we have come to be who we are as children of Earth... she who continues to give us birth and life in ever fuller measure. This is not just about human beings! We are so accustomed to seeing ourselves as the centre of created life and its pinnacle that our hubris blinds us to the reality of who we really are and what our true place is in the created universe. Details of this story we have heard in a simplified version in the story of The Woman with the Lost Coin when a human muses in the presence of a garden frog.

It is this story that gives us the context for all other stories, including the stories we have just read. Without this story, there would be no other stories at all. It is only within this Earth, this universe that any story can be born. And it is only in this context can we hear the stories of the Gospels.

A conversation between Sophia, Earth and the Human...

Human: We all need stories to tell us who we are, to help us find meaning in the world around us and meaning in our lives. We, as human beings, are very familiar with story. We have been aware of its power and used it in all ages and across cultures.

Earth: But we have our own story and it is one that includes all you humans whatever your culture. It is bigger than any of your stories, past or present. It encompasses all forms of life, including what you call 'inanimate' things! It's the story of how the universe came into being.

Sophia: For a long time now, you Christians have based your search for wisdom on a limited story... The redemption story... It has been a tale of escape from the world, seeing eternal life somewhere outside this world. In more recent times some of you have picked up another entrancing story... the scientific story... with its focus on controlling the physical world and using it as an object for your benefit.

Earth: Neither of these stories is enough on their own to give you sufficient meaning and understanding of your journey. And, just as importantly, they can't provide the energy you need to take the directions that will continue to give life and a future to the whole Earth community.

Human: Yes, many of us are still enamoured with the redemption story... as if the primary revelation is that we are sinners and Jesus came to 'save' us... but this message has little relevance to our presence and activity on this planet today.

Earth: It has blinded you to the natural world from which you have emerged and to which you belong.

Sophia: And it creates a 'religious' world that remains separate from and irrelevant to the rest of humanity and the Earth itself. It blinds you to the real implications and connections between your actions and their effects on other human beings and Earth.

It encourages those who have a religious sentiment to live in a bubble and isolates them from the very source of life and meaning which is their heritage. You humans may be a gift to Earth but even more so, Earth is gift to you, and the source of all your life and meaning.

Human: Others of us are captivated by the scientific view of the world. We are caught up in an endless search to control natural processes and the very DNA of life itself. It directs our energies in a way that does not adequately call forth from us a deep respect and compassion for the rest of the created world. Sometimes we lose sight of the sacredness of Earth.

Sophia: Up to the present, the scientific and the religious views in isolation and the behaviour that goes with each one, is not serving you well. They follow the patriarchal principle of binary thinking, one's right and the other is wrong, creating polar positions pitted against each other. Such thinking doesn't help the enrichment and expansion of human thought and experience.

The believing community remains tied to a focus on a Saviour, on the individual human and their safe passage to the next life, and on their own specific members.

They may see things as somehow made in the image of the divine... but it is in a fixed manner. It does not see the world as a 'continually emerging process' of which they are a part, but not the only part. [1]

Earth: Traditional believers of all cultures remain caught in this world view. The underside of it is that faith communities remain disconnected as communities from their intrinsic membership in the community of life. They see themselves as being outside and superior to this broader community of Earth. And so they miss the very truth of who they are as kin to all that has been created and what this relationship asks of them.

All your Gospel stories need to be read and heard in this context of connection and communion with the whole.

Sophia: Listen, people, open yourselves to what is being made known to you. You are Earth coming to self-consciousness. This gives you incredible power, far beyond other earth creatures. Wake up to what is being asked of you! There is no 'opt out' option here. The future is increasingly in your hands. What future do you want for yourselves, your children and grandchildren? Wake up! You are creating it now!

Human: "O God of my ancestors and Lord of mercy... With you is wisdom, she who knows your works and was present when you made the world; she understands what is pleasing in your sight... Send her forth from the holy heavens and from the throne of your glory send her, that she may labour at my side, and that I may learn what is pleasing to you. For she knows and understands all things and she will guide me wisely in my actions..." (Wisdom 9:1,9-11)

BIBLIOGRAPHY

Beavis, Mary Ann (ed.)

The Lost Coin. Parables of Women, Work and Wisdom, Sheffield Academic Press. London. 2002.

Berry, Thomas

*The Dream of the Earth.*Sierra Club Books. San Francisco. 1988.

Crumlin, Rosemary (ed.)

Beyond Belief, Modern Art and the Religious Imagination, National Gallery of Victoria. 1998.

Getty-Sullivan, Mary Ann.

Parables of the Kingdom, Jesus and the Use of Parables in the Synoptic Tradition, Liturgical Press, Collegeville, Minnesota. 2007.

Herzog II, William R.

Parables as Subversive Speech. Jesus as Pedagogue of the Oppressed, John Knox Press. Louisville. Kentucky. 1994.

Johnson, Elizabeth.

Truly our Sister. A Theology of Mary in the Communion of Saints, Continuum. New York. 2003.

Quest for the Living God. Continuum. New York. 2007

Abounding in Kindness. Orbis Books. New York. 2015.

Levine, Amy-Jill (ed).

A Feminist Companion to Mark, Sheffield Academic Press England 2001.

A Feminist Companion to Luke, Sheffield Academic Press England 2002.

Reid, Barbara.

Choosing the Better Part. Women in the Gospel of Luke, The Liturgical Press. Minnesota. 1996.

Parables for Preachers Year C, The Liturgical Press. Minnesota. 2000.

Parables for Preachers Year A, The Liturgical Press. Minnesota. 2001.

Schneiders, Sandra.

Written That You May Believe.Encountering Jesus in the Fourth Gospel, The Crossroads Publishing Company. New York. 1999, 2003

Schussler-Fiorenza, Elisabeth.

In Memory of Her. A Feminist Theological Reconstruction of Christian Origins, Crossroad. New York.1990.

But She Said. Feminist Practices of Biblical Interpretation, Beacon Press. Boston.1992.

Tolbert, Mary Ann.

Perspectives on the Parables: An Approach to Multiple Interpretations, Fortress Press, Philadelphia. 1979.

Wainwright, Elaine.

Towards a Feminist Critical Reading of the Gospel According to Matthew, Walter de Gruyter. New York. 1991.

Shall We Look for Another? A Feminist Rereading of the Matthean Jesus. Orbis Books. New York.1998

Women Healing/Healing Women: The Genderization of Healing in Early Christianity, Equinox Publishing Ltd. London. 2006.

Habitat, Human, and Holy. An Eco-Rhetorical Reading of the Gospel of Matthew, Sheffield Phoenix Press. 2016.

END NOTES

Preface

1. Kiki Smith, in Rosemary Crumlin (ed.), *Beyond Belief: Modern Art and the Religious Imagination*, Melbourne, National Gallery of Victoria, 1998, p. 180.
2. Elizabeth Johnson, *Abounding in Kindness*, Maryknoll, NY, Orbis Books, 2015, p. 146.

Introduction

1. Elisabeth Schűssler Fiorenza, *But she said*, Boston, Mass., Beacon Press, 1992, pp. 50 and 198.
2. Ibid, p. 101.
3. Elizabeth Johnson, YouTube, Mary Magdalene, 3 May 2015.
4. Ibid.

Foremothers

1. Veronica Lawson, personal communication, 2018.
2. Elizabeth Johnson, *Truly Our Sister*, New York, Continuum, 2003, p.223.
3. Elaine Wainwright, Towards a Feminist Critical Reading of the Gospel According to Matthew, Berlin, De Gruyter, 1991, p.68.
4. "...it's not Joseph who begets, but Mary who gives birth," Johnson, *Truly Our Sister*, p. 225.
5. Wainwright, Towards a Feminist Critical Reading of the Gospel According to Matthew, p. 71.

Annunciation

1. Johnson, *Truly Our Sister*, p. 239.

The Meeting of Mary and Elizabeth

1. The text of the *Magnificat* is taken from *The People's Companion to the Breviary*, Indianapolis, The Carmelites of Indianapolis, 1997.

2. Elizabeth Johnson, *Quest for the Living God*, New York, Continuum, 2003, p. 82.
3. Johnson, Truly Our Sister, p. 272.

Nativity

1. The era of the early fathers of the church date c. 150-610.
2. Elizabeth Johnson, *Abounding in Kindness*, Maryknoll, NY, Orbis Books, 2015, p. 222.

Anna the Prophet

1. Barbara Reid, *Choosing the Better Part*, Collegeville MN, Liturgical Press, 1996, p. 94.
2. The Reform Jewish High Holy Days prayer book *MishkanHaNefesh*, released in 2015includes a version of *Avinu Malkeinu* that refers to God as both "Loving Father" and "Compassionate Mother."

Sung versions of *Avinu Malkeinu* can be found on you tube.

The Daughter of Jairus

1. Elaine Wainwright, *Women Healing/Healing Women*, Abingdon, Routledge, 2014, p. 116.

The Bleeding Woman

1. Amy-Jill Levine, *A Feminist Companion to Mark*, Cleveland, OH, Pilgrim Press, 2005, p. 77.
2.Wainwright, Women Healing/Healing Women, p. 120.
3. Ibid, p. 123.

The Widow of Nain

1. Reid, Choosing the Better Part, p. 106.
2. Johnson, Abounding in Kindness, p. 47.

Call of the Mother-in-Law of Peter

1. Wainwright, Women Healing/Healing Women, p. 144.
2. Ibid, p. 146.

Mary and Martha

1. Barbara Reid, *Wisdom's Feast*, Grand rapids, Eerdmans, 2016, p.107.
2. Schűssler Fiorenza, *But She Said*, p. 68.

Martha Professes Her Faith

1. Sandra Schneiders, *Written That You May Believe*, New York, Crossroad, 2003, p. 174.
2. Ibid, p. 107.

The Widow's Mite

1. Reid, Choosing the Better Part, p. 197.

The WomanBent Over

1. Schűssler Fiorenza, *But She Said*, p. 199.
2. Elisabeth Schűssler Fiorenza, *In Memory of Her*, New York, Crossroad, 1983, p. 125.

The Woman with the Lost Coin

1. Linda Maloney, 'Swept Under the Rug' in Mary Ann Beavis (ed.), *The Lost Coin*, London, Sheffield Academic Press, 2002, p.34.
2. Johnson, Quest for the Living God, p. 106.

Canaanite Woman

1. Elaine Wainwright, Shall *We Look for Another?*, Maryknoll, NY, Orbis Books, 1998, p. 87.

Woman's Persistence for Justice

1. W.R.Herzog, *Parables as Subversive Speech*, Westminster John Knox Pres, 1994, pp. 215-218; Barbara Reid, *Parables for Preachers Year C*,Collegeville MN, Liturgical Press, 2000, p. 228.
2. Reid, *Wisdom's Feast*, p 48.
3. Reid, Parables for Preachers Year C, p. 233.

A Woman Anoints Jesus

1. E. Wainwright, Towards a Feminist Critical Reading of the Gospel According to Matthew, p 269.

Women Witnesses of the Crucifixion

1. Wainwright, Towardsa Feminist Critical Reading of the Gospel According to Matthew, p. 142.

Mary Magdalene at the Tomb

1. Schneiders, *Written That You May Believe*, pp. 213-214.
2. Ibid, p.217.

Epilogue

1. This conversation is an adaptation from Thomas Berry, *Dream of the Earth*, Sierra Club Book, 1990, p. 129.

www.ingramcontent.com/pod-product-compliance
Lightning Source LLC
Chambersburg PA
CBHW060521010526
44107CB00060B/2650

* 9 7 8 0 6 4 8 5 6 6 1 8 2 *